Crochet Collage
GARDEN

100 patterns for crochet flowers, plants and petals

CHRIS NORRINGTON

DAVID & CHARLES

www.davidandcharles.com

Contents

Introduction 4

Tools and Materials 10

Collages 12

Woodland Glade 14

Spring Awakening 24

Cottage Garden 34

Vintage Blue Bouquet 44

Midsummer Daydream 54

Flower Meadow 64

Terracotta Pot 74

Poppy Posy 84

Autumn Wreath 94

Midwinter Magic 104

Techniques 114

General Information 116

Crochet Stitches 117

Embroidery Stitches 121

Other Techniques 122

More Inspiration 124

About the Author 126

Acknowledgements 126

Yarn Suppliers 126

Index 127

Introduction

Two of my favourite pastimes are gardening and crochet, and writing this book has allowed me to combine the two.

I was interested in gardening and growing things from a very early age. I was given a packet of candytuft seeds as a child, and I can remember my delight when they actually grew into flowers. I was hooked from then on, much encouraged by the excellent examples set for me by my parents, and particularly my grandparents, who were all enthusiastic gardeners. Now, I'm lucky enough to have a garden of my own, on the edge of the beautiful North York Moors National Park, and I can grow flowers, fruit and vegetables to my heart's content. I am constantly inspired by the colours, shapes and textures in the garden, and they provide most of the ideas for my creative work.

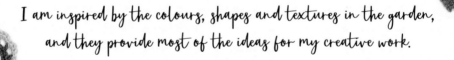

I am inspired by the colours, shapes and textures in the garden, and they provide most of the ideas for my creative work.

And now for the crochet part of the story! I have always been a knitter, taught by my grandmother when I was about seven years old. Skip forward to ten years ago, and I remember seeing a colourful crocheted granny square blanket at a local vintage fair and being fascinated by it. I decided it was time to teach myself to crochet! It was the start of a wonderful creative journey for me, not only learning new skills, but making new friends along the way. Once I'd learned the basic stitches, I started finding new ways to use crochet.

My love of gardening inevitably led me to want to crochet flowers and leaves, and I began to combine them together to create pictures, or collages. Again, I think this has its roots in my childhood. I always loved playing with those little felt shapes that magically 'stuck' onto a background board, creating an endless variety of scenes. Now, I'm doing the same thing, but using crocheted shapes! I started an Instagram account to share my crochet creations, and discovered a whole new crochet community.

My love of gardening inevitably led me to want to crochet flowers and leaves, and I began to combine them together to create pictures, or collages.

This book contains 10 crocheted collages, each providing 10 different motifs, all inspired in some way by my garden. They roughly follow the pattern of the seasons in my part of the world, and so also represent a year in my Yorkshire garden, from the first flowers in spring, through to the frosty leaves of winter. You may recognise some of the flowers and leaves as actual, real-life plant species, but many are imaginary, loosely based on shapes or colours found in my garden, but are not intended to be botanically accurate representations of particular plants. Alongside the more usual front-on views of flowers, I have included some patterns for flowers viewed from the side, half-opened flowers, buds, seedheads, berries and fungi. There is also a large variety of foliage types, from individual leaves to leafy stems, ferns and grasses.

There are endless possibilities for using and combining the motifs, and I hope this book will provide you with many happy hours of creative time.

You may recognise some of the flowers and leaves as actual, real-life plant species, but many are imaginary, loosely based on colours or shapes found in my garden.

I have included some patterns for flowers viewed from the side, half-opened flowers, buds, seedheads, berries and fungi.

Tools and Materials

YARNS

FIBRES

Personally, I love to use yarns made from natural fibres to create my botanical motifs. The different textures can be used to good effect to recreate the characteristics of certain plants more accurately.

I like the stitch definition and texture of cotton yarns, and there is a fantastic range of colours available. Fibres such as alpaca and mohair are perfect for giving a slightly fluffy texture. Mercerised cotton yarns have a lovely sheen that catches the light, and so can be a good choice for petals. Pure wool and alpaca yarns also have the benefit of having a natural springiness and a tendency to curl, which can be exploited when making flowers, as the petals will tend to curl naturally to give a slightly 3D effect.

Occasionally I use two yarns with contrasting textures held together, perhaps a 4-ply cotton to give some structure and rigidity alongside a very delicate lace weight mohair for fluffy texture. It's fun to experiment and try different combinations to see what works best, or which yarns you prefer working with.

Of course, the types of yarn that you use will be your own personal choice, and the motifs can be made using your own favourite fibres and brands of yarn.

YARN QUANTITIES

Most of the patterns use only very small amounts of yarn, so I have not given indications of quantities. These motifs are a great way to use up even very small oddments of yarn. I have a basket of tiny balls of leftover yarn from other projects, ideal for dipping into when I want to make a few flowers.

HOOKS

I use Clover Amour hooks, which have very comfortable grip handles, as I find they reduce the tension that can build up in my hands when crocheting lots of small, intricate items. There are many other types of hook available.

I have indicated the particular yarns I used to create the elements for each collage, and the hook size I used, so if you wish to replicate the collages exactly, you will be able to do so. However, these are just examples and not requirements. You can use any yarns you have available but just make sure you use the hook size that is recommended for your chosen yarn.

A note about size and scale

The type of yarn and hook you choose will determine the size of your finished motif, so no dimensions are given. In this example, I have crocheted the same leaf pattern (this one is from the Midwinter Magic collage) in various yarns, using the appropriate hook size for each type of yarn, from 6mm down to 2.5mm. You could crochet a whole collage using chunky yarn and a large hook, to create a large wall hanging. Alternatively you could go to the opposite end of the scale and work the motifs using fine crochet cotton and a tiny hook, to create a miniature collage. It's entirely up to you...have fun and experiment!

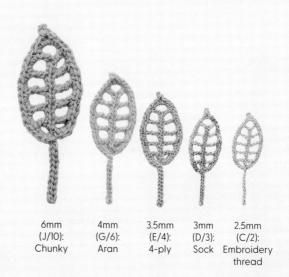

| 6mm
(J/10):
Chunky | 4mm
(G/6):
Aran | 3.5mm
(E/4):
4-ply | 3mm
(D/3):
Sock | 2.5mm
(C/2):
Embroidery
thread |

Collages

Woodland Glade

This collage is inspired by a sun-dappled, shady corner in my garden. In late winter, the dark green shoots and graceful white bells of the first snowdrops start to emerge, followed shortly after by the pale yellow petals of the primroses. Ferns grow very happily in the damp shade, and it's always a joy to see their fronds slowly unfurling as the days grow gradually longer and warmer. Shy little violets peep out from underneath piles of logs, and clumps of tiny pale toadstools pop up here and there. Pretty pale green and dusky pink hellebores also make a welcome appearance. Twisting stems of ivy wind their way up the tree trunks and patches of mottled green lichen grow slowly amongst mossy tree roots. When the sun shines through the new leaves in the spring, it is a magical little corner of the garden.

THE MOTIFS

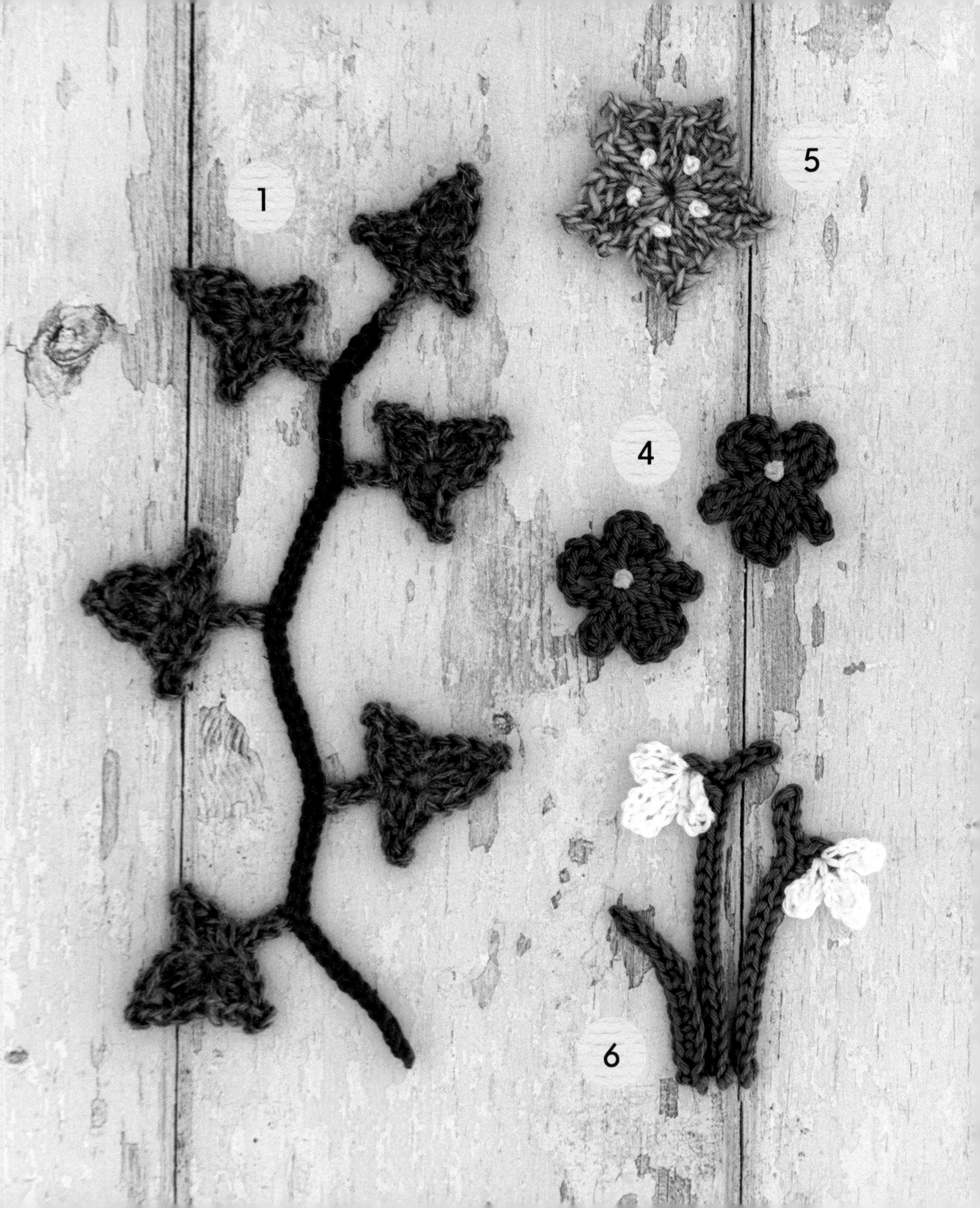

1 I've used...

+ **Yarn A:** Drops Safran 4-ply cotton
+ **Yarn B:** Drops Alpaca
+ 3mm (D/3) hook

STEM

Using Yarn A (Brown), work ch stitches until stem is of desired length, skip 1 ch, slst back along chain. Fasten off Yarn A.

LEAF

Using Yarn B (Green) and with RS facing, slst into stem ch at the place where you want to position your leaf.

Round 1: 10 ch, skip 6 ch, join with slst in 7th ch from hook to make a ring.

Round 2: Pass yarn under ring, slst into the ring, then work the following stitches into the ring: (1 htr, 1 tr, 3-ch picot, 1 tr, 1 htr), slst, 1 htr, 1 tr, 1 dtr, 3-ch picot, 1 dtr, 1 tr, 1 htr, slst, repeat instructions in round brackets once more, slst in original 7th ch, slst in remaining 3 leaf stem chs, slst in stem.

Fasten off and weave in ends.

Add more leaves as required along both sides of the main stem. If you vary the intervals between the leaves, it will give a more natural effect.

SPECIAL STITCH

3-ch picot: Work 3 ch, skip 2 ch, slst in 1 ch.

2 I've used...

+ **Yarn A:** Drops Safran 4-ply cotton
+ **Yarn B:** DMC Petra No 3 crochet cotton
+ 3mm (D/3) hook

Using Yarn A (Orange), make a magic ring.

Round 1: 1 ch (counts as 1 dc), 9 dc in ring. Join with slst in beg 1-ch, pulling Yarn B (Yellow) through.

Round 2: 4 ch, 1 dtr into st at base of beg ch, [1 tr, 1 dtr, 4 ch, slst] in next dc, *[slst, 4 ch, 1 dtr] in next dc, [1 tr, 1 dtr, 4 ch, slst] in next dc, repeat from * 3 more times.

Fasten off and weave in ends.

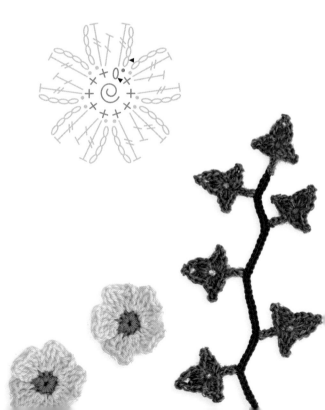

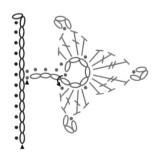

I've used...

+ **Yarns A and B:** Drops Baby Alpaca Silk
+ 3mm (D/3) hook

CAP

Using Yarn A (Cream), make a magic ring.

Row 1 (RS): 3 ch (counts as 1 tr), 3 tr in ring, 3 ch (counts as 1 tr), turn.

Row 2: 1 tr in st at base of 3 ch, 1 tr in 2 tr, 1 tr in top of 3 ch, 1 ch (does not count as 1 dc), turn.

Row 3: 2 dc in next 4 tr, 2 dc in top of 3 ch. Fasten off Yarn A.

STEM

With WS facing, attach Yarn B (Brown) with a slst in the back of the central dc from Row 3.

Row 1: Work 15 ch, skip 1 ch, slst back along ch, slst in back of same dc.

Fasten off and weave in ends.

Note: *To give a natural effect, make mushrooms with stems of varying lengths, so there are taller and shorter ones within a group.*

I've used...

+ **Yarn A:** Patons Cotton DK
+ **Yarn B:** Drops Flora (wool/alpaca blend)
+ 3.5mm (E/4) hook

Using Yarn A (Purple), make 5 ch, join with slst in first ch to make a ring.

Round 1: Working over the yarn tail, ([3 ch, 1 tr, 3 ch, slst] in ring) twice, [7 ch, slst] in ring, [4 ch, 1 dtr, 4 ch, slst] in ring, [7 ch, slst] in ring.

Fasten off. Gently pull yarn tail to close centre hole.

Using Yarn B (Yellow) or embroidery cotton, work a French knot at the base of the top two petals.

Fasten off and weave in ends.

5 *I've used...*

- **Yarn A:** Scheepjes Catona 4-ply cotton or Drops Delight Print 4-ply sock yarn
- Oddments of contrasting 4-ply cotton for the French knots
- 3.5mm (E/4) hook

Using Yarn A (Pink), make 6 ch, join with slst in first ch to form a ring.

Round 1: Working over the yarn tail, ([4 ch, 1 dtr, 2 ch, slst in 2nd ch from hook, 1 dtr, 4 ch, slst] in ring) 5 times. Pull gently on the yarn tail to help close the centre hole.

Fasten off and weave in ends.

Using a contrasting colour of 4-ply cotton, work several French knots into the central area.

6 *I've used...*

- **Yarn A:** Ricorumi Cotton
- **Yarn B:** Patons Cotton 4-ply
- 3mm (D/3) hook

STEM

Using Yarn A (Green), make 18 ch, slst in 4th ch from hook.

Row 1: 4 ch, skip 1 ch, slst in remaining 17 stem chs.

FLOWER

Using Yarn B (White), join with slst in 4-ch ring.

Round 1: Working into ring, 3 ch, 1 tr, 3 ch, slst, 4 ch, 1 dtr, 4 ch, slst, 3 ch, 1 tr, 3 ch, slst. Fasten off and weave in ends.

LEAF

Using Yarn A (Green), make 12 ch, skip 1 ch, slst in 3 ch, dc in 6 ch, slst in 2 ch.

Fasten off and weave in ends.

To make flowers that face in the opposite direction, simply reverse the stem instructions as follows: 18 ch, skip 1 ch, slst in 3 ch, 4 ch, slst in 4th ch from hook, slst in remaining stem chs. The number of starting chs can be varied to give taller or shorter stems.

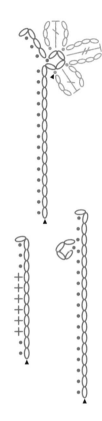

7 *I've used...*

+ **Yarn A:** Drops Safran 4-ply cotton
+ 3mm (D/3) hook

STEM

Using Yarn A (Green), make 10 ch.

Large leaf 1: (5 ch, 3tr-cl in 4th ch from hook) twice, 3 ch, slst in 3rd ch from hook, (3 ch, slst in ch at base of 3tr-cl, slst in 1 ch) twice.

3 ch for stem.

Large leaves 2 and 3: As large leaf 1, 3 ch for stem.

Small leaf 1: *5 ch, 3tr-cl in 4th ch from hook, 3 ch, slst in 3rd ch from hook, 3 ch, slst in ch at base of 3tr-cl, slst in 1 ch**, 3 ch for stem*.

Small leaf 2: Repeat small leaf 1 from * to *.

Small leaf 3: Repeat small leaf 1 from * to **.

Top leaf and other side of fern: Work as for small leaf from * to ** once more, turn to work down opposite side of ch, (work from * to ** as for small leaf, slst in next 3 stem chs) 3 times, (make large leaf 1, slst in 3 stem chs) 4 times, slst in remaining 7 stem chs.

Fasten off and weave in ends.

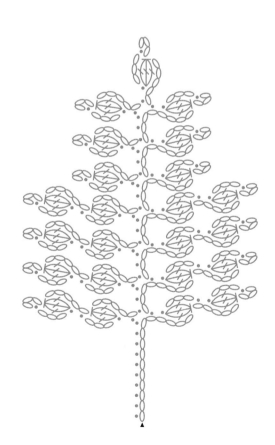

I've used...

+ **Yarn A:** Hedgerow Yarns hand-dyed sock yarn

+ 3mm (D/3) hook

Note: *You may find it helpful to use a stitch marker to mark the beginning of each round, although stitch numbers are really not critical. We are aiming to make an organic shape, so slight variations are not a problem.*

Using Yarn A (Green), make a magic ring.

Round 1: 8 dc in ring, join with slst in first dc. Pull yarn tail to close the ring.

Round 2: 1 ch (does not count as a st throughout) 2 dc in each dc around, slst in beg 1-ch. Place marker.

Round 3: 1 ch, (3 dc in dc, 3 tr in dc) 8 times, join with slst in beg 1-ch. Place marker.

Round 4: 3 ch, (2 tr in next 3 dc, 2 tr in next 3 tr) 4 times, 2 ch, slst in last tr worked into from Round 3.

Fasten off and weave in ends.

Note: *The piece of lichen will naturally want to curl over to give a double-layer effect. There is no need to block, as the slightly ruffled texture is exactly the effect we want.*

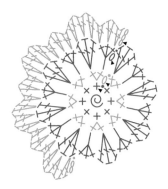

 I've used...

+ **Yarn A:** Scheepjes Catona 4-ply cotton

+ **Yarn B:** Drops Safran 4-ply cotton

+ 3.5mm (E/4) hook

Using Yarn A (Dark Green), 4 ch, join with slst into a ring.

Round 1 (RS): Working into the ring, 5 ch, 1 htr, 2 ch, 1 tr, 2 ch, 1 dtr, 2 ch, 1 dtr, 2 ch, 1 tr, 2 ch, 1 htr, 4 ch, slst in first ch of beg 5-ch. Fasten off Yarn A.

Round 2: With RS facing, and using Yarn B (Light Green), slst in 5ch-sp, 1 ch, [2 dc, 2 htr, 2 tr] in 5ch-sp, 3 tr in 2ch-sp, 4 tr in 2ch-sp, [2 tr, 2 ch, slst in 2nd ch from hook, 2 tr] in 2ch-sp, 4 tr in 2ch-sp, 3 tr in 2ch-sp, [2 tr, 2 htr, 2 dc] in last 2ch-sp, slst in beg 1-ch.

Row 3 (stem): 7 ch, skip 1 ch, slst in 6 ch, slst in beg ch of Round 2.

Fasten off and weave in ends.

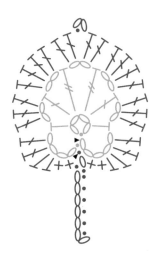

I've used...

+ **Yarn A:** King Cole Merino Blend DK
+ 4mm (G/6) hook

Using Yarn A (Green), make 10 ch.

Large leaves: (8 ch, slst in 8th ch from hook, 3 ch for stem) 3 times.

Middle leaves: (6 ch, slst in 6th ch from hook, 3 ch for stem) 3 times.

Small leaves: (4 ch, slst in 4th ch from hook, 3 ch for stem) twice.

Leaf tip: (4 ch, slst in 4th ch from hook) 3 times.

Working down the opposite side of ch, slst in 3 stem ch.

Small leaves: (4 ch, slst in 4th ch from hook, slst in 3 stem ch) twice.

Middle leaves: (6 ch, slst in 6th ch from hook, slst in 3 stem ch) 3 times.

Large leaves: (8 ch, slst in 8th ch from hook, slst in 3 stem ch) twice, 8 ch, slst in 8th ch from hook, slst in remaining 10 ch for stem.

Fasten off and weave in ends.

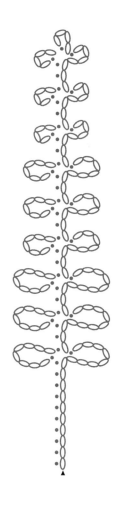

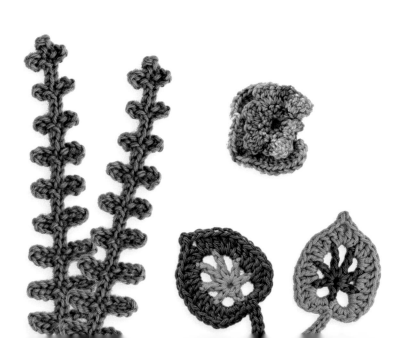

Spring Awakening

Spring is a wonderful time of year, full of promise and new life. In my garden, everything seems to burst suddenly into life, the new leaves are a fresh vibrant green and long-awaited colour fills the borders as daffodils, grape hyacinths and forget-me-nots come into flower. Soft fluffy buds appear on the pussy willow and catkins dangle from the hazel branches. Amongst all of this yellow, blue and green, the first buds of blossom appear on the apple trees, adding a lovely touch of pink.

I love to pick flowers to bring inside, and at this time of year my home is usually filled with colourful bunches of flowers in pretty vases.

THE MOTIFS

5

1

8

9

6

1 *I've used...*

+ **Yarn A:** 4-ply cotton
+ Oddments of 4-ply cotton or embroidery thread for the French knots
+ 3mm (D/3) hook

Using Yarn A (Blue), make a magic ring.

Round 1: 5 dc in ring, slst in first dc.

Round 2: (2 ch, 2tr-cl in same st, 2 ch, slst in next dc) 5 times working the last slst into slst at end of Round 1. Fasten off Yarn A.

CENTRE

Using 4-ply cotton or embroidery thread, make a French knot in the centre of the flower.

Fasten off and weave in ends.

2 *I've used...*

+ **Yarn A:** Drops Merino Extra Fine
+ **Yarn B:** Drops Safran 4-ply cotton
+ 3mm (D/3) or 3.5mm (E/4) hook

Round 1: Using Yarn A (Blue), make 11 ch, skip 3 ch, slst in 8 ch, 1 ch.

Round 2: Working up the other side of the original ch, slst in first ch, (2 ch, skip 1 ch, dc in 1 ch, skip 1 ch on main stem, slst in 1 ch) 3 times, (2 ch, skip 1 ch, dc in 1 ch, slst in 3ch-sp) twice, working down the other side of the flower, (slst in next slst, 2 ch, skip 1 ch, dc in 1 ch, skip 1 slst) 4 times, slst in ch at the base of the flower. Fasten off Yarn A.

STEM

Join Yarn B (Green) with slst in ch at base of flower, work chs to make desired length of stem.

Fasten off and weave in ends.

I've used...

+ **Yarns A and B:** Drops Safran 4-ply cotton
+ 3.5mm (E/4) hook

I've used...

+ **Yarns A and B:** Drops Safran 4-ply cotton
+ 3mm (D/3) or 3.5mm (E/4) hook

CENTRE OF FLOWER

Using Yarn A (Orange), make 5 ch, join with a slst in first ch to form a ring.

Round 1 (RS): 2 ch (counts as 1 htr), 11 htr in ring, working over the yarn tail, join with slst in FLO of 2nd ch. Tip: It's helpful to put a stitch marker in the back loop of this chain. Pull the yarn tail gently to help close the centre ring.

Round 2: 1 ch (counts as 1 dc), 1 dc in FLO of 11 htr, join with slst in first ch.

Round 3: (3 ch, slst in next dc) 11 times. 3 ch, slst in last slst of Round 2. Fasten off Yarn A.

OUTER PETALS

Round 1: With RS facing, and working in the back loops of the htrs from Round 1, join Yarn B (Yellow) with a slst in the back loop of the ch where you placed your stitch marker, 4 ch, skip 1 htr, (slst in BL of next htr, 3 ch, skip 1 htr) 5 times, skip 1 htr, slst in first ch of beg 4-ch.

Round 2: Slst in 4ch-sp, [1 htr, 1 tr, 1 dtr, 1 trtr, 2 ch, skip 1 ch, slst in 1 ch, 1 trtr, 1 dtr, 1 tr, 1 htr] in 4ch-sp, then in each 3ch-sp around (6 petals made), join with slst in last slst of Round 1.

Fasten off Yarn B. Weave in all ends.

Using Yarn A (Green), make a magic ring.

Row 1 (RS): 3 ch (counts as 1 tr), 3 tr in ring, 3 ch, turn. Do not fully close the magic ring if you wish to add a stem later.

Row 2: 1 tr in st at base of 3 ch, 1 tr in 2 tr, 1 tr in top of 3-ch, turn.

Row 3: (4 ch, slst in next tr) 3 times. Fasten off Yarn A.

Row 4: With RS facing, join Yarn B (Yellow) with slst in first of 4 ch, 7 ch, skip 1 ch, slst in 1 ch, [2 dtr, 1 tr, slst] in first 4ch-sp, [slst, 1 htr, 1 tr, 1 dtr, 1 trtr, 2 ch, skip 1 ch, slst in 1 ch, 1 trtr, 1 dtr, 1tr, 1 htr, slst] in next 4ch-sp, [slst, 1 tr, 2 dtr] in last 4ch-sp, 2 ch, skip 1 ch, slst in 1 ch, 5 ch, slst in last ch of 4-ch from Row 3. Fasten off Yarn B.

STEM

Add a stem by joining Yarn A (Green) in the magic ring at the base of the flower, ch desired length of stem, fasten off. Gently pull the yarn end of the magic ring to fully close.

Weave in all ends.

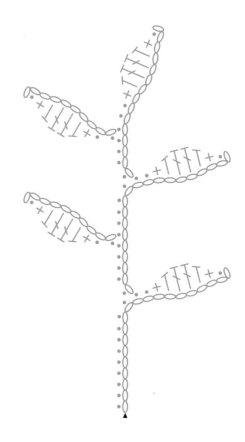

+ **Yarn A:** Drops Muskat DK cotton
+ 4mm (G/6) hook

Round 1 (RS): Using Yarn A (Green), make 12 ch, skip 4 ch, 4dtr-cl in next ch, 4 ch, skip 3 ch, slst in 1 ch, 5 ch, slst in ch at bottom of 4dtr-cl.

Round 2: Pass yarn under stem, 1 ch, [4 dc, 1 htr] in 4ch-sp, [1 htr, 1 tr, 2 ch, skip 1 ch, slst in 1 ch, 1 tr, 1 htr] in 3ch-sp, [1 htr, 4 dc] in 5ch-sp, 1 ch, slst in slst on stem, slst in 6 stem chs.

Fasten off and weave in ends.

+ **Yarn A:** Drops Safran 4-ply cotton
+ 3mm (D/3) hook

STEM

Using Yarn A (Green), make 10 ch.

Make leaf: [10 ch, skip 1 ch, slst, 1 dc, 1 htr, 2 tr, 1 htr, 1 dc, 2 slst along ch].

10 ch for stem, make leaf, 5 ch for stem, make leaf, slst in next stem ch, make leaf, slst in 9 stem chs, make leaf, slst along remaining 15 stem chs.

Fasten off and weave in ends.

7

I've used...

+ **Yarn A:** Scheepjes Catona 4-ply cotton
+ **Yarn B:** King Cole Giza Cotton 4-ply
+ 3mm (D/3) hook

STEM

Using Yarn A (Green), make 14 ch, skip 1 ch, slst in next 2 ch, 1 dc in next ch, 5 ch, skip 1 ch, slst in next 2 ch, 1 dc in next ch, skip 1 ch (creates 1ch-sp to work flower bud into), slst in next 10 ch. Fasten off Yarn A.

FLOWER BUD

Join Yarn B (Pink) with slst in 1ch-sp, 4 ch, 4dtr-cl in 1ch-sp, 2 ch, skip 1 ch, slst in 1 ch, 4 ch, slst in 1ch-sp.

Fasten off Yarn B. Weave in all ends.

 8

I've used...

+ **Yarn A:** Drops Muskat DK cotton
+ **Yarn B:** 1 strand Drops Sky and 1 strand Drops Brushed Alpaca Silk held together
+ 4mm (G/6) hook

STEM

Using Yarn A (Beige), ch sts for desired length of stem, (4 ch, skip 3 ch, slst in 1 ch, 6 ch) 3 times, 4 ch, skip 3 ch, slst in 1 ch, working back down the other side of the stem, slst in 4 ch, (4 ch, skip 3 ch, slst in 1 ch, slst in 6 ch) 3 times, slst in remaining stem chs. Fasten off Yarn A.

BUDS

Using Yarn B (Grey and Fluffy Blue), make a bud by working this sequence of sts into each 4ch-sp, [slst, 2 ch, 3tr-pc, 2 ch, slst].

Fasten off and weave in ends (see Techniques: Other Techniques for sewing in multiple tail ends).

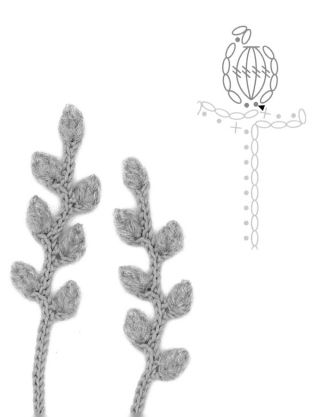

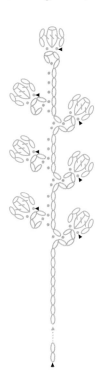

I've used...

+ **Yarns A and B:** Drops Safran 4-ply cotton

+ 3.5mm (E/4) hook

STEM

Using Yarn A (Brown), ch number of sts required to give desired length of stem, 4 ch, skip 3 ch, slst in 1 ch to make first loop, *10 ch for stem, 4 ch, skip 3 ch, slst in 1 ch to make second loop, 3 ch, skip 1 ch, slst back along all stem chs. Fasten off Yarn A.

***Note:** if making several stems, you can vary the number of chains between the two groups of catkins, to give a more natural look.*

CATKINS

Catkin 1: Join Yarn B (Yellowy Green) with a slst in first 4ch-sp, 7 ch, skip 1 ch, 1 dc in 4 ch, slst in 2 ch, slst in 4ch-sp, 9 ch, skip 1 ch, 1 dc in 5 ch, slst in 3 ch. Fasten off.

Catkin 2: Join Yarn B with slst in 2nd 4ch-sp, 7 ch, skip 1 ch, 1 dc in 4 ch, slst in 2 ch, slst in 4ch-sp, 9 ch, skip 1 ch, 1 dc in 6 ch, slst in 2 ch, slst in 4ch-sp, 6 ch, skip 1 ch, 1 dc in 2 ch, slst in 3 ch.

Fasten off and weave in all ends.

***Note:** Stem can be reversed to have the catkins hanging from the other side. Chain number of stitches for total desired length of item, skip 1 ch, slst in 2 ch, 4 ch, skip 3 ch, slst in 1 ch (makes 2nd loop), slst in 10 ch, 4 ch, skip 3 ch, slst in 1 ch (makes first loop), slst in remaining stem chs. Follow instructions for Catkin 1 and Catkin 2 for adding the catkins.*

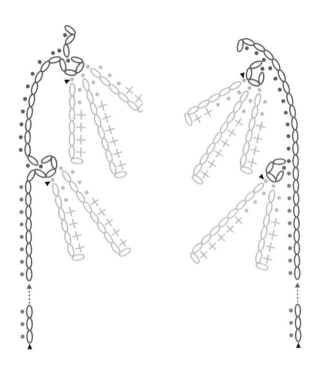

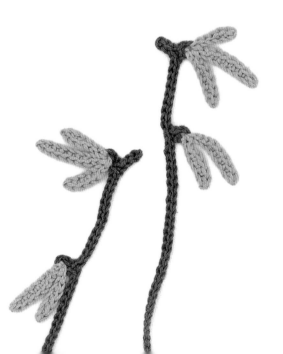

10 *I've used...*

+ **Yarn A:** Drops Muskat DK cotton
+ Oddments of 4-ply yarn or embroidery cotton to decorate
+ 4mm (G/6) hook

Using Yarn A (Cream), make 15 ch.

Row 1 (RS): Skip 1 ch, 1 dc in 14 ch, 1 ch, turn. (14 dc)

Row 2: 1 dc in 14 dc, 1 ch, turn.

Row 3: 2 dc in first dc, 1 dc in 12 dc, 2 dc in last dc, 1 ch, turn. (16 dc)

Row 4: 1 dc in 16 dc, 1 ch, turn.

Row 5: 2 dc in first dc, 1 dc in 14 dc, 2 dc in last dc, 1 ch, turn. (18 dc)

Row 6: 1 dc in 18 dc, 1 ch, turn.

Row 7: 2 dc in first dc, 1 dc in 16 dc, 2 dc in last dc, 1 ch, turn. (20 dc)

Row 8: 1 dc in 20 dc, 1 ch, turn.

Rows 9–14: Same as Row 8.

Row 15: Dc2tog, 1 dc in 16 dc, dc2tog, 1 ch, turn. (18 dc)

Row 16: 1 dc in 18 dc, 1 ch, turn.

Row 17: Dc2tog, 1 dc in 14 dc, dc2tog, 1 ch, turn. (16 dc)

Row 18: 1 dc in 16 dc, 1 ch, turn.

Row 19: Dc2tog, 1 dc in 12 dc, dc2tog, 1 ch, turn. (14 dc)

Row 20: 1 dc in 14 dc, 1 ch, turn.

Row 21: Dc2tog, 1 dc in 10 dc, dc2tog, 1 ch, turn. (12 dc)

Row 22: 1 dc in 12 dc, 1 ch, turn.

Row 23: 1 dc in 12 dc.

Fasten off and weave in ends.

DECORATION

Using oddments of 4-ply yarn or embroidery cotton, and using the photograph as a guide, stitch flowers and leaves using lazy daisy stitch, chain stitch, straight stitch and French knots. This is just a suggestion: feel free to create your own decoration inspired by the colour scheme or flowers you have chosen for your vase.

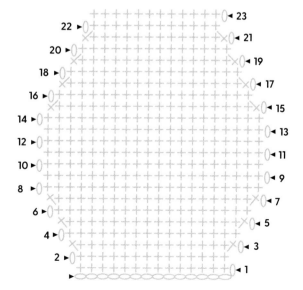

Cottage Garden

This collage evokes a summer herbaceous border, filled with old-fashioned cottage garden plants. I love this style of gardening, with all the flowers growing closely together, in a slightly haphazard and tangled way, so that the borders appear to be overflowing. I have lots of tall plants, such as hollyhocks, foxgloves and campanulas in my garden, some I have nurtured from seeds, others just appear each year in different places as if by magic. Ox-eye daisies are always a delight, poking out between their taller neighbours. Sweet-scented roses and peonies add soft pink and apricot pastel shades in amongst the bolder colours. Summer annuals grow near the fence, alongside the soft greenery of herbs.

6

8

5

2

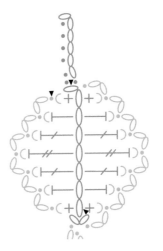

 1

I've used...

+ **Yarn A:** Drops Merino Extra Fine
+ **Yarn B:** Drops Safran 4-ply cotton
+ 3.5mm (E/4) hook

LARGE FLOWER (MAKE 2)

Using Yarn A (Blue), make a magic ring, leaving a 20cm (8in) tail (to use later for stitching the flower to the stem).

Row 1 (WS): 3 ch (counts as 1 tr), 3 tr in ring, 3 ch, turn.

Row 2: 1 tr in next 2 tr, 1 tr in top of 3-ch, 3 ch, turn. (4 tr)

Row 3: Slst in same st, (3 ch, slst in next tr) twice, 3 ch, slst in top of 3-ch from Row 2. Fasten off and weave in ends.

SMALL FLOWER (MAKE 2)

Using Yarn A, make a magic ring, again leaving a 20cm (8in) tail.

Row 1 (RS): 3 ch (counts as 1 tr), 3 tr in ring, 3 ch, turn.

Row 2: Slst in same st, (3 ch, slst in next tr) twice, 3 ch, slst in top of 3-ch from Row 1. Fasten off Yarn A.

STEM

Using Yarn B (Green), make a simple stem (see Techniques: Other Techniques). Using the photo as a guide, stitch the flowers in position with a few tiny stitches using the yarn tails.

Fasten off and weave in all ends.

2

I've used...

+ **Yarn A:** Drops Baby Alpaca Silk
+ **Yarn B:** Drops Brushed Alpaca Silk
+ 3.5mm (E/4) hook

Using Yarn A (Blue), make 8 ch.

Round 1 (RS): Skip 1 ch, 1 dc in 1 ch, 1 htr in 1 ch, 1 tr in 1 ch, 1 dtr in 1 ch, 1 tr in 1 ch, 1 htr in 1 ch, 1 dc in last ch, 2 ch, working back along the other side of the starting ch, 1 dc, 1 htr, 1 tr, 1 dtr, 1 tr, 1 dc, slst in beg 8th ch (turning ch). If a stem is required, 6 ch, skip 1 ch, slst in 5 ch, slst in 8th ch (turning ch) to finish. Fasten off Yarn A.

Round 2: Join Yarn B (Pale Blue) with slst in BLO of first dc of Round 1, [2 ch, slst in BLO of next st] 6 times, slst in 2ch-sp, 3 ch, skip 2 ch, slst in 1 ch, slst in 2ch-sp, [2 ch, slst in BLO of next st] 7 times, 2 ch, slst in 8th ch (turning ch).

Fasten off Yarn B and weave in all ends.

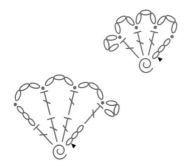

3 I've used...
+ **Yarns A and B:** 4-ply cotton
+ 2.5mm (C/2) hook

Using Yarn A (Yellow), make a magic ring.

Round 1: 1 ch (counts as 1 dc), 5 dc in ring, join with slst in first ch, pulling Yarn B (White) through.

Round 2: (3 ch, skip 1 ch, slst in 2 ch, slst in next dc) 5 times, fasten off invisibly (see Techniques: Crochet Stitches – Invisible Join).

Weave in all ends.

4 I've used...
+ **Yarn A:** 4-ply cotton
+ 3.5mm (E/4) hook

Using Yarn A (Green), make 10 ch for stem (can be varied).

1st Leaf: 9 ch, skip 3 ch, 1 tr in 1 ch, 1 htr in 2 ch, 1 dc in 2 ch, slst in 1 ch, 3 ch for stem.

2nd Leaf: 8 ch, skip 3 ch, 1 tr in 1 ch, 1 htr in 2 ch, 1 dc in 1 ch, slst in 1 ch, 3 ch for stem.

3rd Leaf: 6 ch, skip 2 ch, 1 htr in 2 ch, 1 dc in 1 ch, slst in 1 ch, 3 ch for stem.

4th Leaf: 5 ch, skip 2 ch, 1 htr in 1 ch, 1 dc in 1 ch, slst in 1 ch.

5th Leaf: As 4th leaf, slst in 3 stem chs.

6th Leaf: As 3rd leaf, slst in 3 stem chs.

7th Leaf: As 2nd leaf, slst in 3 stem chs.

8th Leaf: As 1st leaf, slst in remaining stem chs.

Fasten off and weave in ends.

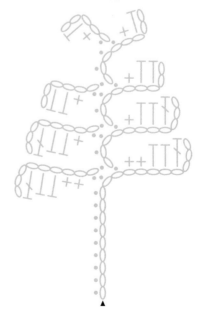

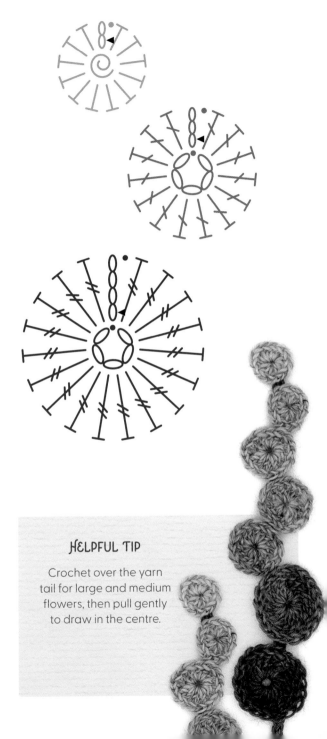

I've used...

+ **Yarn A:** Drops Delight Print 4-ply sock yarn
+ 3.5mm (E/4) hook

LARGE FLOWER (MAKE 2)

Using Yarn A (Pink), make 5 ch, join with slst in first ch to make a ring.

Round 1 (RS): 4 ch, 18 dtr in ring, fasten off invisibly (see Techniques: Crochet Stitches – Invisible Join) in top of beg 4-ch.

MEDIUM FLOWER (MAKE 2)

Using Yarn A, make 5 ch, join with slst in first ch to make a ring.

Round 1 (RS): 3 ch, 14 tr in ring, fasten off invisibly in top of beg 3-ch.

SMALL FLOWER (MAKE 2)

Using Yarn A, make a magic ring.

Round 1 (RS): 2 ch, 12 htr in ring, fasten off invisibly in top ofbeg 2-ch.

TO COMPLETE

Make a simple straight stem (see Techniques: Other Techniques). Using the photo as a guide, arrange the flowers from the smallest at the top to the largest. Attach to the stem by using a dab of PVA glue, or a couple of tiny stitches with matching sewing thread.

Weave in all ends.

HELPFUL TIP

Choosing a yarn with a gradual colour change will give the effect of the natural variations in flower colours. You can create the same effect by choosing three slightly different shades of the same yarn, for example, a dark, medium and light pink.

HELPFUL TIP

Crochet over the yarn tail for large and medium flowers, then pull gently to draw in the centre.

6 *I've used...*

- + **Yarn A:** DMC 4-ply cotton
- + **Yarn B:** Drops Baby Alpaca Silk
- + **Yarn C:** Drops Alpaca
- + 3.5mm (E/4) hook

Using Yarn A (Yellow), make 6 ch, join with slst in first ch to make a ring.

Round 1 (RS): Working over yarn tail, 3 ch (counts as 1 tr), 11 tr in ring, join with slst in FLO of 3rd ch, pulling Yarn B (Pale Pink) through. Pull yarn tail gently to draw centre closed. Fasten off Yarn A. Tip: It's helpful to place a stitch marker in the back loop of the 3rd ch, to mark the place where Round 3 starts.

Round 2: Using Yarn B (Pale Pink), and working in FLO of trs, (2 ch, 3 tr in next 2 tr, 2 ch, slst in 1 tr) 4 times. Fasten off Yarn B.

Round 3: Join Yarn C (Mid Pink) in the BLO of the 3rd ch from Round 1 (where you placed your stitch marker if used). Hold the petals from Round 2 towards you, and work in the BLO of the trs from Round 1, (3 ch, 4 dtr in next 2 tr, 3 ch, slst in 1 tr) 4 times. Fasten off Yarn C.

Weave in all ends. I prefer not to block this flower, as the petals will curl naturally. A quick spray with starch or stiffener will hold the petals in place.

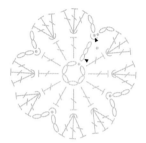

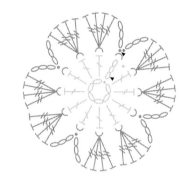

7 *I've used...*

- + **Yarn A:** Drops/Ricorumi Cotton yarns
- + **Yarn B:** Drops Muskat DK cotton/Drops Alpaca/Drops Soft Tweed
- + 4mm (G/6) hook

Round 1 (RS): Using Yarn A, 10 ch (can be varied to give longer/shorter stem), skip 3 ch, [4 tr, 3 ch, slst] in 1 ch, slst in remaining stem chs. Fasten off Yarn A.

Round 2: With RS facing, join Yarn B with slst in first tr, 1 ch, 1 htr in same tr, 2 htr in 3 tr, 1 ch, slst in top of 3-ch. Fasten off Yarn B.

Weave in all ends.

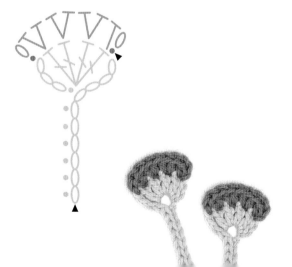

8 *I've used...*

+ **Yarns A and B:** Various 4-ply cotton yarns
+ 3.5mm (E/4) hook

Using Yarn A (Light Green), make 12 ch.

Round 1 (RS): Skip 1 ch, 1 dc in 11 ch. Place working loop on a stitch marker. Do not cut yarn.

Round 2: With RS facing, join Yarn B (Dark Green) with slst in first ch from Round 1, 1 dc in 1 ch, 1 htr in 2 ch, 1 tr in 1 ch, 1 dtr in 3 ch, 1 tr in 2 ch, 1 htr in 1 ch, [1 dc, 2 ch, 1 dc] in turning ch then work the following sts into the BLO of the dcs down the other side of the leaf, 1 htr in 1 dc, 1 tr in 2 dc, 1 dtr in 3 dc, 1 tr in 1 dc, 1 htr in 2 dc, 1 dc in 1 dc, slst in BLO of final dc. Fasten off Yarn B.

BORDER

Remove stitch marker, and continuing with Yarn A, 1 ch, 1 dc in 12 sts, [1 dc, 2 ch, skip 1 ch, slst in 1 ch, 1 dc] in 2ch-sp, 1 dc in 12 sts, 1 ch, slst in beg 1 ch.

STEM

6 ch, skip 1 ch, slst in 5 ch, slst in beg 1 ch at base of leaf.

Fasten off Yarn A and weave in all ends.

 9 *I've used...*

+ **Yarn A:** Drops Safran 4-ply cotton
+ 3.5mm (E/4) hook

Using Yarn A (Green), make 14 ch for stem.

Make leaf: 7 ch, skip 1 ch, 1 dc in 6 ch, pass yarn under work, 1 ch, slst in first of original 7 ch, 1 dc in 1 ch, 1 htr in 1 ch, 1 tr in 1 ch, 1 htr in 1 ch, 1 dc in 1 ch, slst in original 7th ch (turning ch), 3 ch, skip 2 ch, slst in 1 ch, 1 dc in dc, 1 htr in 1 dc, 1 tr in 1 dc, 1 htr in 1 dc, 1 dc in 1 dc, slst in 1 dc, slst in 1 ch.

Slst in 2 stem chs, 16 ch for stem, make leaf, slst in 6 stem chs, 4 ch for stem, make leaf, slst in remaining stem chs.

Fasten off and weave in ends.

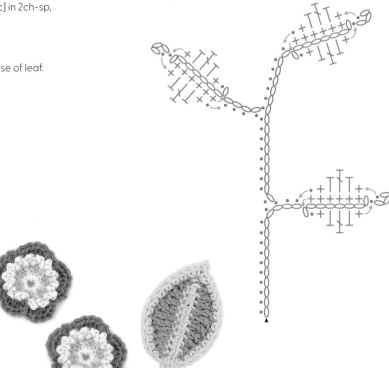

I've used...

- **Yarns A, B and C:** Various combinations of Drops Baby Alpaca Silk/Drops Alpaca
- Oddments of contrasting yarn for the French knots
- 3.5mm (E/4) hook

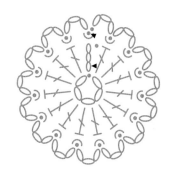

Using Yarn A (Orange), make 5 ch, join with slst in first ch to make a ring.

Round 1 (RS): Working over yarn tail, 3 ch (counts as 1 tr), 14 tr in ring, join with slst in FLO of 3rd ch. Pull yarn tail gently to draw centre closed. Tip: It's helpful to place a stitch marker in the back loop of the 3rd ch, to mark the starting point for Round 3.

Round 2 (Front layer of petals): Working in FLO of trs from Round 1, (3 ch, slst in FLO of next tr) 14 times, 3 ch, slst in slst. Fasten off Yarn A invisibly (see Techniques: Crochet Stitches – Invisible Join).

Round 3 (Back layer of petals): Join Yarn B (Cream) with slst in BLO of 3rd ch from Round 1 (where you placed your stitch marker if used), 3 ch, (5 tr in BLO of 1 tr, 3 ch, slst in BLO of 1 tr, slst in BL of 1 tr, 3 ch) 4 times, 5 tr in BLO of 1 tr, 3 ch, slst in 1 tr, slst in base of beg 3-ch.

Fasten off Yarn B.

Centre details: Using contrasting 4-ply yarn or embroidery thread, and using the photo as a guide, work a few French knots around the centre of the flower.

Fasten off and weave in all ends.

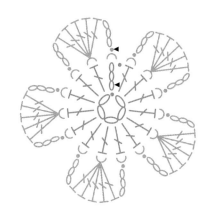

Vintage Blue Bouquet

For this collage I have drawn inspiration from lots of different plants and flowers in my garden, including the beautiful shapes and soft pastel colours of candytuft and scabious. Delicate lily-of-the-valley, periwinkle and clematis, as well as seedheads and stems of leafy foliage, come together to make up a very pretty bouquet. The container for these blooms is a beautiful bowl, which is a modern take on the decorative patterns on traditional blue and white crockery. I have picked out my favourite shades of blues, purples and greens, but you could very easily adapt this collage to create your own bouquet using your favourite colour palette.

1

I've used...

+ **Yarn A:** 1 strand Patons Cotton 4-ply/ 1 strand King Cole Bamboo Cotton 4-ply held together with 1 strand Drops Kid-Silk
+ 3.5mm (E/4) hook

Using Yarn A (Lavender), make 5 ch, join with slst in first ch.

Round 1: 3 ch (counts as 1 tr), 14 tr in ring, working over the yarn tail. Join with slst in top of 3-ch. Pull yarn tail gently to draw centre hole closed.

Round 2: (3 ch, slst in next tr) 14 times. 3 ch, slst in slst.

Fasten off Yarn A.

Centre details: Thread a length of contrasting yarn into a yarn needle. Work several straight stitches from centre outwards to represent stamens.

Fasten off and weave in all ends.

2

I've used...

+ **Yarn A:** Scheepjes Catona 4-ply cotton
+ **Yarns B and C:** Drops Muskat DK cotton
+ 4mm (G/6) hook

Using Yarn A (Light Green), make a magic ring.

Round 1: 1 ch (counts as 1 dc), 7 dc in ring, join with slst in FLO of first ch.

Round 2: (2 ch, slst in 2nd ch from hook, slst in FLO of next dc) 8 times. Fasten off Yarn A.

Round 3: Join Yarn B (Blue) with slst in BLO of 1 ch from Round 1, 3 ch, 1 tr in same st, working in BLO, 2 tr in next 7 dc, join with slst in top of beg 3-ch, pulling Yarn C (Light Blue) through.

Round 4: Continuing with Yarn C, *3 ch, 2 tr in 1 tr, ** slst in 1 tr, repeat from * 6 more times and from * to ** once, fasten off invisibly (see Techniques: Crochet Stitches – Invisible Join).

Centre details: Thread a length of contrasting colour yarn into a yarn needle, and use to work a French knot in the centre of the flower. Bring the yarn up through the centre, wrap yarn round needle 3 times, take the needle back down through the centre.

Fasten off and weave in all ends.

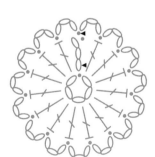

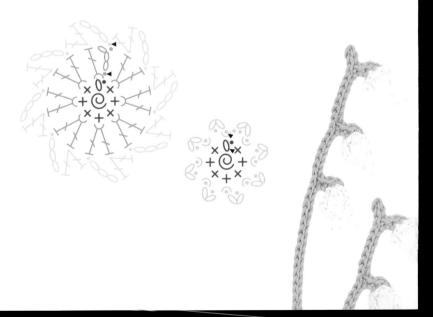

3 I've used...

+ **Yarns A and B:** Drops Safran 4-ply cotton
+ 3mm (D/3) hook

STEM

Using Yarn A (Green), make 25 ch.

Row 1: Slst in 4th ch from hook, slst in 1 ch, (12 ch, slst in 4th ch from hook, slst in 1 ch) twice, 3 ch, skip 1 ch, slst in every ch back along length of stem. Fasten off Yarn A.

FLOWER

With RS facing, join Yarn B (White) with slst in the first 3ch-sp on the stem.

Row 1: 4 ch, 3tr-cl in 3ch-sp, 3 ch, skip 1 ch, slst in 2 ch, 2 ch, skip 1 ch, slst in 2 ch, 4 ch, slst in 3ch-sp.

Fasten off and weave in ends.

Make another flower in each of the remaining 3ch-sps.

Note: *The stem can be reversed so that the flowers hang from the other side, as follows:*
38 ch, skip 1 ch, slst in 3 stem chs, (5 ch, skip 3 ch, slst in 2 ch, slst in 7 stem chs) 3 times, slst along remaining 20 stem chs. Fasten off. Add the flowers as before.

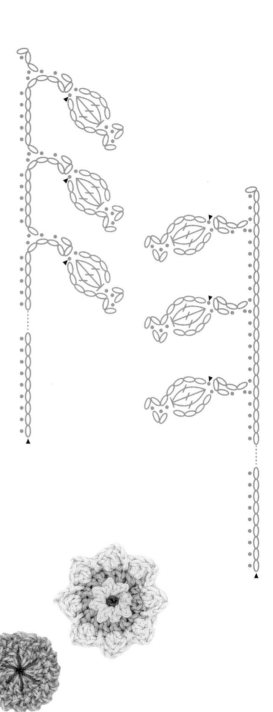

4 *I've used...*

+ **Yarn A:** Scheepjes Catona 4-ply cotton
+ 3.5mm (E/4) hook

Using Yarn A (Green), make 5 ch, join with slst in first ch.

Round 1: Working into ring, 7 ch, 1 tr, 4 ch, 1 tr, 4 ch, 1 dtr, 4 ch, 1 tr, 4 ch, 1 tr, 6 ch, slst in first ch of beg 7-ch.

Round 2: 1 ch, [2 dc, 4 htr, 2 dc] in 7ch-sp, [1 dc, 1 htr, 2 tr, 1 htr, 1 dc] in first 4ch-sp, [1 dc, 1 htr, 2 tr, 2 dtr] into 2nd 4ch-sp, 2 ch, skip 1 ch, slst in 1 ch, [2 dtr, 2 tr, 1 htr, 1 dc] into 3rd 4ch-sp, [1 dc, 1 htr, 2 tr, 1 htr, 1 dc] into 4th 4ch-sp, [2 dc, 4 htr, 2 dc] into 6ch-sp, slst in first ch.

Work ch sts to make length of stem desired, skip 1 ch, slst back along remaining stem chs, slst in beg ch at base of leaf.

Fasten off and weave in ends.

5 *I've used...*

+ **Yarn A:** Drops Safran 4-ply cotton
+ **Yarns B and C:** Drops Muskat DK cotton
+ 3.5mm (E/4) and 4mm (G/6) hooks

STEM

Using Yarn A (Green) and smaller hook, make 22 ch, skip 4 ch, slst in 5 ch, 9 ch, skip 4 ch, slst in 18 ch. Fasten off.

FLOWER

Using Yarn B (Blue) and larger hook, slst in first 4ch-sp.

Row 1 (RS): 3 ch (counts as 1 tr), 6 tr in 4ch-sp. Fasten off Yarn B.

Row 2: With RS facing, using Yarn C (Light Blue), slst in top of 3-ch from Row 1, 3 ch, 2 tr in 1 tr, ([slst, 3 ch, 2 tr] in 1 tr) twice, slst in last tr.

Fasten off and weave in ends.

Work a flower in the second 4ch-sp in the same way.

6 *I've used...*

+ **Yarn A:** Scheepjes Catona 4-ply cotton
+ 3.5mm (E/4) hook

Using Yarn A (Light Green), make 10 ch.

Note: *The number of chain stitches can be varied to create the desired length of stem.*

1st Branch: 13 ch, MS, slst in 3 ch, 5 ch, MS, slst in 7 ch.

2nd Branch: 22 ch, MS, slst in 4 ch, 7 ch, MS, slst in 7 ch.

3rd Branch: 12 ch, MS, slst in 5 ch, 7 ch, MS, slst in 3 ch, 10 ch, MS, slst in 10 ch.

4th Branch: Slst in 5 ch, 10 ch, MS, slst in 3 ch, 7 ch, MS, slst in remaining chs of stem.

Fasten off and weave in ends.

SPECIAL STITCH

MS (Make Seed): Skip 3 ch, [3 tr, 1 dc] in 1 ch.

 7 *I've used...*

+ **Yarn A:** Patons Cotton DK
+ **Yarn B:** Drops Muskat DK cotton
+ 3.5mm (E/4) hook

Using Yarn A (Dark Blue), make a magic ring.

Round 1: 1 ch (counts as 1 dc), 7 dc in ring, join with slst in first ch, pulling through Yarn B (Mid Blue).

Round 2: Continuing with Yarn B, 4 ch, 1 dtr in same st, [1 dtr, 4 ch, slst] in 1 dc, *[slst, 4 ch, 1 dtr] in 1 dc, [1 dtr, 4 ch, slst] in 1 dc, repeat from* twice.

Fasten off and weave in ends.

Note: *The petals will curl slightly. You can spray them with starch or stiffener to hold their shape, or block if desired.*

8 *I've used...*

+ **Yarn A:** Drops Flora (wool/alpaca blend) or Drops Alpaca
+ 3mm (D/3) hook

Using Yarn A (Pale Blue), make 5 ch for stem.

Make leaf: [6 ch, skip 4 ch, 3tr-cl in 1 ch, 2 ch, skip 1 ch, slst in 1 ch, 5 ch, slst in original 5th ch, slst in 1 ch].

*5 ch, make leaf, repeat from * 3 times (5 leaves made in total), 1 ch for stem, make leaf, (make leaf, slst in 5 stem chs) 5 times.

Fasten off and weave in ends.

9 *I've used...*

+ **Yarn A:** Drops Muskat DK cotton
+ **Yarn B:** Rico Essentials Organic Cotton Aran
+ 4mm (G/6) hook

Using Yarn A (Blue), make 5 ch, join with slst in first ch to make a ring.

Round 1: 1 ch (counts as 1 dc), 7 dc in ring, join with slst in first ch.

Round 2: 4 ch, 2 dtr in same st, [2 dtr, 4 ch, slst] in 1 dc, *[slst, 4 ch, 2 dtr] in 1 dc, [2 dtr, 4 ch, slst] in 1 dc, repeat from * twice. Fasten off Yarn A.

Round 3: Join Yarn B (White) with extended slst between any two petals and into centre ring, 1 ch, *4 dc in 4ch-sp, 1 dc in 1 dtr, 1 htr in 1 dtr, 2 ch, skip 1 ch, slst in 1 ch, 1 htr in 1 dtr, 1 dc in 1 dtr, 4 dc in 4ch-sp,** extended slst into centre ring, repeat from * twice, and from * to ** once more, slst in first ch.

Fasten off Yarn B and weave in ends.

10 I've used...

+ **Yarn A:** Rico Essentials Organic Cotton Aran
+ **Yarn B:** DK cotton
+ **Yarn C:** 4-ply cotton
+ 4mm (G/6) hook

Using Yarn A (White), make 20 ch, turn.

Row 1 (RS): Skip 1 ch, 1 dc in each st, 1 ch (does not count as a st), turn. (19 sts)

Rows 2–4: Repeat Row 1, but at end of Row 4, work 3 ch (does not count as a st) instead of 1 ch, turn.

Row 5: 2 tr in 1 dc, 1 tr in 17 dc, 2 tr in 1 dc, 3 ch, turn. (21 sts)

Row 6: (2 tr in 1 tr) twice, 1 tr in 17 tr, (2 tr in 1 tr) twice, 3 ch, turn. (25 sts)

Row 7: 1 tr in each tr, 3 ch, turn. (25 sts)

Row 8: 2 tr in 1 tr, 1 tr in 23 tr, 2 tr in 1 tr, 3 ch, turn. (27 sts)

Row 9: 1 tr in each tr, 3 ch, turn. (27 sts)

Row 10: 1 tr in each tr, 1 ch, turn. (27 sts)

Row 11: 1 dc in each tr. Fasten off.

DECORATION

Using Yarn B (Blue) and a yarn needle, and using the photograph as a guide, work a row of chain stitches across the base of the bowl, along Row 4 of the crochet.

Work a row of vertical straight stitches, across Rows 1 to 3 of the crochet.

Work a row of chain stitches across the top of the bowl (between rows 10 and 11 of the crochet).

Using Yarn C (Light Blue) or embroidery cotton, work flowers using lazy daisy stitch, and add French knot centres.

Fasten off and weave in all ends.

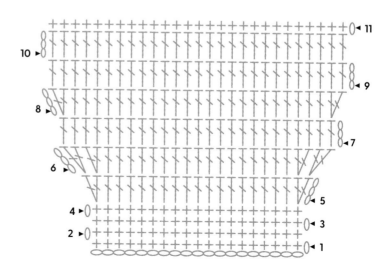

Midsummer Daydream

It's a warm, sunny midsummer day in the garden, and there's nothing better than lying in the grass, looking up at the sky with the flower stems arching overhead and tall grasses waving gently in the breeze...this collage is inviting you to take a moment, and enjoy a midsummer daydream!

Some of the flowers are based on real summer favourites, such as delicate pale pink and white cosmos, and the beautiful, tall, mustard yellow flowers of fennel. Others are purely imaginary – a fantasy floral meadow of pretty flowers and foliage.

I was also inspired by some of the shapes, colours and patterns used in traditional folk art paintings.

6

10

2

7

5

I've used...

+ **Yarn A:** Drops Alpaca/Drops Safran 4-ply cotton
+ **Yarn B:** King Cole Giza Cotton 4-ply
+ 3mm (D/3) hook

Using Yarn A (Yellow), make 5 ch, join with slst in first ch to make a ring.

Round 1 (RS): 1 ch (counts as a st), 7 dc in ring, join with slst in FLO of first ch.

Round 2: (2 ch, slst in FLO of next dc) 8 times. Fasten off Yarn A.

Round 3: Join Yarn B (Pale Pink) with slst in BL of first dc of Round 2, (10 ch, skip 4 ch, 1 tr, 1 dtr, 2 tr, 1 htr, 1 dc along chain, slst in BLO of next dc) 8 times, finishing with a slst in BLO of first dc.

Fasten off and weave in ends.

I've used...

+ **Yarn A:** Scheepjes Catona 4-ply cotton
+ **Yarn B:** Wendy DK Cotton
+ 3.5mm (E/4) hook

Using Yarn A (Green), make a magic ring.

Round 1 (RS): 3 ch, 4 tr, 3 ch, slst in ring. Do not fully tighten the magic ring if you'd like to add a stem later. Fasten off Yarn A.

Round 2: With RS facing, join Yarn B (Pink), with slst in first tr, (8 ch, skip 3 ch, 1 tr, 1 dtr, 1 tr, 1 htr, 1 dc, slst in next tr) 3 times, 8 ch, skip 3 ch, 1 tr, 1 dtr, 1 tr, 1 htr, 1 dc, slst in last tr. Fasten off Yarn B.

STEM

Join Yarn A with slst in magic ring, ch number of sts required to give desired length of stem, fasten off. Pull the original yarn tail to fully close the magic ring, and fasten off.

Weave in all ends.

3 *I've used...*
+ **Yarn A:** Drops Safran 4-ply cotton
+ 3mm (D/3) hook

Using Yarn A (Yellow), make 20 ch for stem.

Make leaf: [7 ch, skip 4 ch, 2 dtr in 1 ch, 4 ch, slst in ch at base of 2 dtr, slst in 2 ch].

(6 ch, make leaf) twice, 2 ch, make leaf, slst in 4 ch, make leaf, (slst in 8 ch, make leaf) twice, slst in remaining stem chs.

Fasten off and weave in ends.

4 *I've used...*
+ **Yarn A:** Ricorumi Cotton/ Scheepjes Catona 4-ply cotton
+ **Yarn B:** Drops Safran 4-ply cotton
+ 3.5mm (E/4) hook

Using Yarn A (Blue), make 12 ch, join with slst in first ch to make a ring.

Round 1 (RS): 1 ch, 15 dc in ring, join with slst in first ch.

Round 2: 3 ch, skip 1 dc (1 tr in 1 dc, skip 1 dc, 2 ch) 3 times, [1 dtr, 3 ch, 1 dtr] in 1 dc, (2 ch, skip 1 dc, 1 tr in 1 dc) 3 times, 3 ch, skip 1 dc, slst in original slst, pulling Yarn B (Pale Blue) through.

Round 3: Continuing with Yarn B, 1 ch, [2 dc, 2 htr, 1 dc] in 3ch-sp, (*1 dc, 2 htr, 1 dc in 2ch-sp*) 3 times, [1 dc, 1 htr, 3 ch, skip 2 ch, slst in 1 ch, 1 htr, 1 dc] in 3ch-sp, repeat from * to * 3 times, [1 dc, 2 htr, 2 dc] in 3ch-sp, slst in first ch, 5 ch, skip 1 ch, slst in 4 ch, slst in beg 1-ch at base of leaf.

Fasten off and weave in ends.

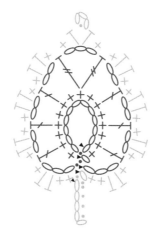

I've used...

+ **Yarn A:** Scheepjes Catona 4-ply cotton
+ **Yarn B:** Drops Alpaca
+ **Yarn C:** Drops Safran 4-ply cotton
+ 3.5mm (E/4) hook

Using Yarn A (Pale Green), make 10 ch (can be varied to create length of stem required).

Make leaf: [9 ch, skip 3 ch, 1 tr in 2 ch, 1 htr in 2 ch, 1 dc in 1 ch, slst in 1 ch].

10 ch, skip 3 ch, slst in 7 ch, make leaf, slst in remaining 10 stem chs. Fasten off Yarn A.

FLOWER

Row 1: With WS facing, join Yarn B (Red) with slst in 3ch-sp at top of stem, 3 ch, 5 tr in 3ch-sp, 4 ch, turn.

Row 2 (RS): (3tr-cl in 1 tr, skip 1 tr, 1 ch) twice, 3tr-cl in 1 tr, 4 ch, slst in 3rd ch of 3 ch on Row 1. Fasten off Yarn B.

Row 3: With RS facing, join Yarn C (Orange) with slst in 4ch-sp, 1 dc in same space, *[1 htr, 1 tr, 1 htr] in 3tr-cl, slst in 1ch-sp, repeat from * once, [1 htr, 1 tr, 1 htr] in 3tr-cl, [1 dc, slst] in 4ch-sp.

Fasten off Yarn C and weave in all ends.

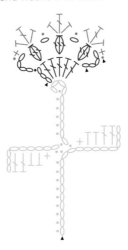

I've used...

+ **Yarn A and Yarn B:** Drops Safran 4-ply cotton
+ **Yarn C:** Drops Alpaca
+ 3mm (D/3) hook

Using Yarn A (Yellow), make a magic ring, 1 ch (counts as 1 dc).

Round 1: 7 dc in ring, join with slst in first ch.

Round 2: 3 ch (counts as 1 tr), 1 tr in same stitch, 1 ch, (2tr-cl in 1 dc, 1 ch) 7 times, join with slst in top of 3-ch. Fasten off Yarn A.

Round 3: Join Yarn B (Pink) with slst in any 1ch-sp from Round 2, 1 ch (counts as 1 dc), 2 dc in same 1ch-sp, 1 ch, (3 dc in 1ch-sp, 1 ch) 7 times. Join with slst in beg 1-ch. Fasten off Yarn B.

Round 4: Join Yarn C (Pale Blue) with slst in any 1ch-sp from Round 3, 1 dc in same space, (3 ch, 1 dc in 1ch-sp) 7 times, 3 ch, join with slst in first dc.

Round 5: Work [slst, 1 htr, 1 tr, 1 htr, slst] into each 3ch-sp around. Fasten off Yarn C.

Weave in all ends.

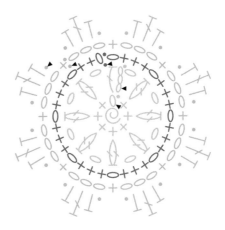

7 *I've used...*

+ **Yarns A and B:** Drops Safran 4-ply cotton
+ Oddments of 4-ply cotton or embroidery cotton for the French knots
+ 3mm (D/3) or 3.5mm (E/4) hook

STEM (RS)

Using Yarn A (Yellow), ch sts for desired length of stem, 5 ch, skip 1 ch, slst in 1 ch, 1 dc in 3 ch, 8 ch, skip 1 ch, slst in 1 ch, 1 dc in 3 ch, skip 3 ch, slst in remaining stem chs. Fasten off Yarn A.

FLOWER

Row 1 (RS): With RS facing, join Yarn B (Purple) with slst in 3ch-sp at top of stem, 1 ch (does not count as a st), 4 dc in same 3ch-sp, 1 ch, turn.

Row 2: 1 dc in 4 dc, 1 ch, turn.

Row 3: 1 dc in 1 dc, 2 dc in next 2 dc, 1 dc in 1 dc, 1 ch, turn. (6 sts)

Rows 4 and 5: 1 dc in 6 dc, 1 ch, turn.

Row 6: 1 dc in 6 dc, 3 ch, turn.

Row 7: 1 tr in base of 3 ch, 1 htr, slst in 1 dc, [slst, 2 ch, 1 tr] in 1 dc, [1 tr, 2 ch, slst] in 1 dc, [slst, 1 htr] in 1 dc, [1 tr, 3 ch, slst] in 1 dc. Fasten off Yarn B.

DECORATION

Using 4-ply cotton or embroidery cotton in a contrasting colour, work a French knot at the base of each top petal.

Weave in all ends.

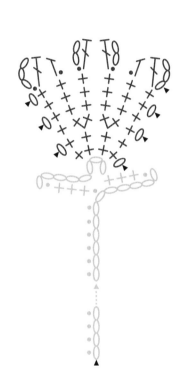

I've used...

+ **Yarn A:** Drops Safran 4-ply cotton
+ **Yarn B:** King Cole Bamboo Cotton 4-ply
+ 3mm (D/3) or 3.5mm (E/4) hook

STEM

Using Yarn A (Green), ch number of sts for desired length of stem, 4 ch, skip 3 ch, slst in 1 ch, 7 ch, skip 3 ch, slst in 1 ch, 5 ch, skip 3 ch, slst in 2 ch, 4 ch, skip 3 ch, slst in 5 ch, 4 ch, skip 3 ch, slst in remaining stem chs. Fasten off Yarn A.

BUDS

Join Yarn B (Purple) with slst in first 4ch-sp, working into the 4ch-sp: [3 ch, 1 tr, 2 ch, slst, 2 ch, 1 htr, 1 ch, slst]. Fasten off here and after each following bud. Make another bud in the same way in the 2nd 4ch-sp. Then work ([slst, 2 ch, 1 htr, 1 ch, slst] into 3rd 4ch-sp) twice, [slst, 1 ch, 1 htr, 2 ch, slst, 2 ch, 1 tr, 3 ch, slst] in the 4th and 5th 4ch-sps.

Fasten off and weave in ends.

HELPFUL TIP

See Techniques: Other Techniques for sewing in multiple tail ends.

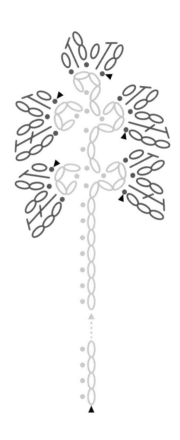

9 *I've used...*

- **Yarn A:** Drops Baby Alpaca Silk
- **Yarn B:** Drops Alpaca/Drops Safran 4-ply cotton
- 3mm (D/3) hook

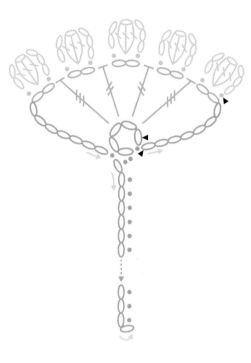

STEM (RS)

Using Yarn A (Beige), 5 ch, join with slst to make a ring, 9 ch, 1 trtr in ring, ([2 ch, 1 dtr] in ring) twice, 2 ch, 1 trtr in ring, 9 ch, slst in ring. Make stem by working chs to desired length, skip 1 ch, slst back along length of stem, slst into ring. Fasten off Yarn A.

SEEDS

With RS facing, and using Yarn B (Yellow), make first seed in the top of the 9ch-sp: [slst, 3 ch, 3tr-pc, 2 ch, slst] into 9ch-sp.

Make another seed in each of the remaining four ch-sps.

Fasten off and weave in ends.

10 *I've used...*

- **Yarn A:** Various cotton yarns
- 3.5mm (E/4) hook

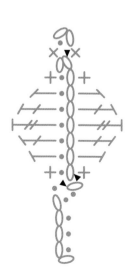

Using Yarn A (Green), make 9 ch, skip 2 ch, slst in 7 ch.

Round 1 (RS): 1 ch, working in the BLO of the foundation ch: 1 dc in 1 ch, 1 htr in 1 ch, 1 tr in 1 ch, 1 dtr in 1 ch, 1 tr in 1 ch, 1 htr in 1 ch, 1 dc in 1 ch, [1 dc, 2 ch, skip 1 ch, slst in 1 ch, 1 dc] in 2ch-sp, working back down the other side of the leaf into the slsts: 1 dc, 1 htr, 1 tr, 1 dtr, 1 tr, 1 htr, 1 dc, slst in beg 1-ch.

Make stem: 5 ch, skip 1 ch, slst in 4 ch, slst in 1 ch at base of leaf.

Fasten off and weave in ends.

Flower Meadow

One of the borders in my garden has been designed as a prairie-style meadow, with ornamental grasses interspersed with tall perennial flowers. The grasses give height, movement and texture, and provide a soft and hazy pale green and gold backdrop for the jewel colours of the flowers. The meadow grows and evolves as the plants spread and self-seed, resulting in surprising combinations and many 'happy accidents'. Flower shape and colour inspirations for this collage come from plants like verbena, echinacea and rudbeckia. My particular favourite is the verbena, with its tall branching airy stems and stunning purple flowers.

10

1

8

7

6

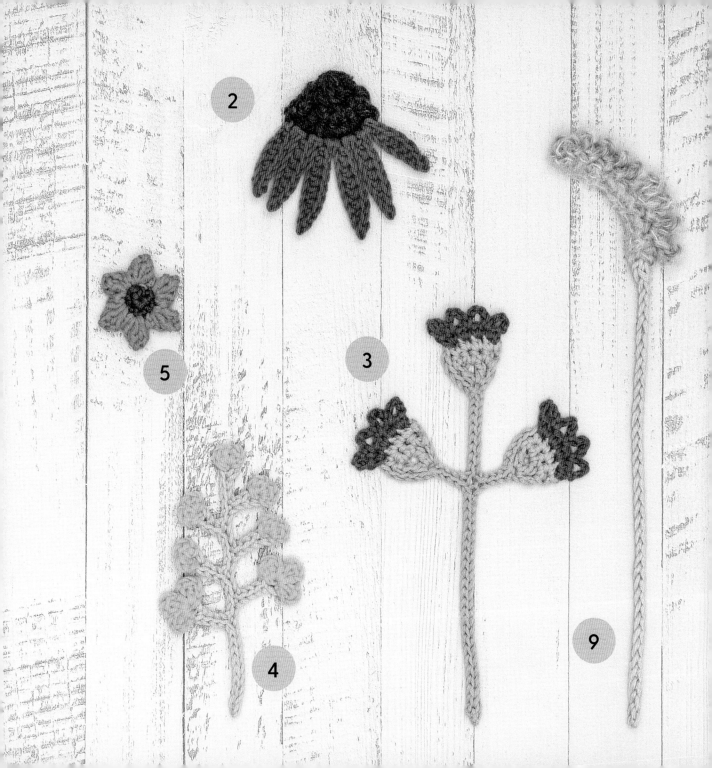

1 I've used...

+ **Yarns A and B:** Drops Safran 4-ply cotton
+ 3.5mm (E/4) hook

Using Yarn A (Yellow), make a magic ring.

Round 1: 3 ch (counts as 1 tr), 13 tr in ring, join with slst in top of 3-ch, pulling Yarn B (Dark Pink) through.

Round 2: Make petal: *4 ch, skip 1 ch, slst in 1 ch, 1 dc in next 2 ch**, slst in next tr, repeat from * 12 more times, and from * to ** once more, fasten off invisibly (see Technique: Crochet Stitches – Invisible Join).

Weave in all ends.

2 I've used...

+ **Yarn A:** Drops Soft Tweed
+ **Yarn B:** Drops Safran 4-ply cotton
+ 3.5mm (E/4) and 4mm (G/6) hooks

Using Yarn A (Dark Red) and larger hook, make a magic ring.

Row 1 (RS): 3 ch (counts as 1 tr), 4 tr in ring, 1 ch, turn.

Row 2: 1 dc in first tr, 2 dc in 3 tr, 1 dc in top of 3-ch, 1 ch, turn.

Row 3: Dc2tog, 1 dc in 4 dc, dc2tog, slst in 1 ch at beg of Row 2. (6 dc)

Fasten off Yarn A.

With RS facing join Yarn B (Bright Pink) in first ch using the smaller hook.

Petal 1: Slst in dc, 7 ch, skip 1 ch, slst, 1 dc, 3 htr, 1 dc, slst in original dc.

Petal 2: Slst in dc, 8 ch, skip 1 ch, slst, 1 dc, 4 htr, 1 dc, slst in original dc.

Petal 3: Slst in dc, 9 ch, skip 1 ch, slst, 1 dc, 5 htr, 1 dc, slst in original dc.

Repeat petal 3 once, then petal 2 once and petal 1 once (6 petals made).

Fasten off Yarn B and weave in all ends.

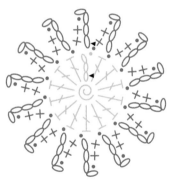

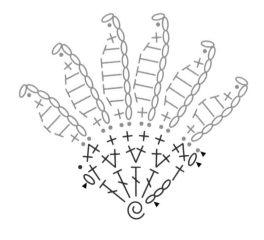

FLOWER MEADOW

68

3   *I've used...*

+ **Yarn A:** Drops Safran 4-ply cotton
+ **Yarn B:** King Cole Bamboo Cotton 4-ply
+ 3mm (D/3) hook

Using Yarn A (Green), ch sts to make a stem of desired length.

BASE FOR FLOWER 1

Row 1 (RS): 8 ch, *[1 tr, 1 ch, 1 tr] in 4th ch from hook, 1 ch, turn.

Row 2: (1 dc in tr, 1 dc in 1ch-sp) twice, 1 ch, turn.

Row 3: 1 dc in each dc, 5 ch, slst in original 4th ch**, slst in 4 ch.

BASE FOR FLOWER 2

Row 1: 13 ch, repeat from * to ** from base for flower 1, slst in 9 ch.

BASE FOR FLOWER 3

Repeat instructions for base for flower 1, slst in remaining stem chs. Fasten off.

PETALS

Row 1 (RS): With RS facing, join Yarn B (Purple) with slst in first dc of Row 3 on base for flower 1, 2 dc in same st, 2 dc in next 3 dc, 4 ch, turn.

Row 2: Slst in 2nd dc, (4 ch, skip 1 dc, slst in next dc) 3 times.

Fasten off and weave in all ends.

HELPFUL TIP

You could easily add extra flowers to this stem, or work a single flower and stem and add to a bouquet collage or arrangement.

4 I've used...

+ **Yarns A and B:** Drops Safran 4-ply cotton
+ 3mm (D/3) hook

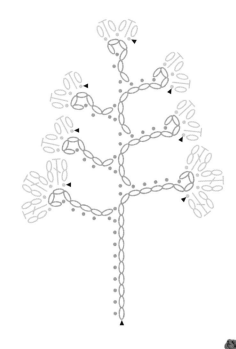

STEM

Using Yarn A (Beige), make 19 ch, slst in 4th ch from hook, slst in 4 ch.

Row 1: 11 ch, slst in 4th ch from hook, slst in 3 ch.

Row 2: 10 ch, slst in 4th ch from hook, slst in 2 ch.

Row 3: 6 ch, slst in 4th ch from hook, slst in 4 ch.

Row 4: 6 ch, slst in 4th ch from hook, slst in 6 ch.

Row 5: 7 ch, slst in 4th ch from hook, slst in 7 ch.

Row 6: 8 ch, slst in 4th ch from hook, slst in remaining 13 ch.

Flowers are worked into the 4ch-sp at the end of each stem, using Yarn B (Golden Yellow).

LOWER 2 FLOWERS

Join Yarn B with slst in 4ch-sp.

Row 1: (2 ch, 1 tr, 2 ch, slst in 4ch-sp) 3 times. Fasten off.

UPPER 5 FLOWERS

Note: *These flowers are worked in the remaining 5 stems.*

Join Yarn B with slst in 4ch-sp.

Row 1: (1 ch, 1 htr, 1 ch, slst in 4ch-sp) twice.

Fasten off and weave in ends.

HELPFUL TIP

As there are several yarn ends with this pattern, here's a tip to make weaving in a bit quicker. From behind, insert hook and pull the last yarn tail through to the back of the flower. Trim both yarn tails to the same length, then thread both at the same time into a yarn needle, and work a couple of back stitches under the back loops of the petals.

5 *I've used...*

- **Yarns A and B:** Drops Muskat DK cotton
- 4mm (G/6) hook

Using Yarn A (Brown), make a magic ring.

Round 1 (RS): 1 ch (counts as dc), 5 dc in ring, join with slst in beg 1-ch. Pull yarn tail to close ring. (6 sts)

Round 2: 1 ch, 1 dc in each dc around, join with slst in beg 1-ch, pulling Yarn B (Orange) through.

Round 3: Continuing with Yarn B, [slst, 2 ch, 3tr-pc, 2 ch, slst in same st] in each dc around.

Fasten off and weave in all ends.

 6 *I've used...*

- **Yarn A:** Drops Alpaca
- 3mm (D/3) hook

Using Yarn A (Green), make 25 ch for stem (can be varied to give desired length).

Make leaf: [4 ch, 4dtr-pc in 4th chain from hook, 4 ch, slst into same 4th ch].

2nd–5th leaves: (4 ch for stem, make leaf) 4 more times.

Working back down other side of ch, [slst in 4 stem chs, make leaf] 4 times. Slst in remaining stem chs.

Fasten off and weave in ends.

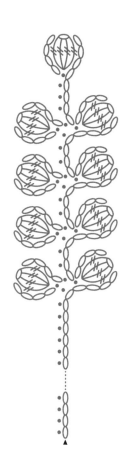

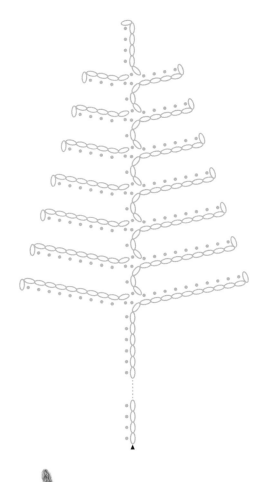

7 *I've used...*

+ **Yarn A:** Drops Baby Alpaca Silk

+ 3mm (D/3) hook

Using Yarn A (Grey Blue), make enough ch sts required for desired length of short base stem.

Row 1: 11 ch, skip 1 ch, slst in 10 ch.

Row 2: 13 ch, skip 1 ch, slst in 9 ch.

Row 3: 12 ch, skip 1 ch, slst in 8 ch.

Row 4: 11 ch, skip 1 ch, slst in 7 ch.

Row 5: 10 ch, skip 1 ch, slst in 6 ch.

Row 6: 9 ch, skip 1 ch, slst in 5 ch.

Row 7: 8 ch, skip 1 ch, slst in 4 ch.

Row 8: 6 ch, skip 1 ch, slst in 5 ch.

Row 9: 5 ch, skip 1 ch, slst in 7 ch (4 slst along the side branch and 3 slst along main central stem).

Row 10: 6 ch, skip 1 ch, slst in 8 ch.

Row 11: 7 ch, skip 1 ch, slst in 9 ch.

Row 12: 8 ch, skip 1 ch, slst in 10 ch.

Row 13: 9 ch, skip 1 ch, slst in 11 ch.

Row 14: 10 ch, skip 1 ch, slst in 12 ch.

Row 15: 11 ch, skip 1 ch, slst along the side branch and all remaining stem chs.

Fasten off and weave in ends.

Pin out carefully and spray with starch or stiffener.

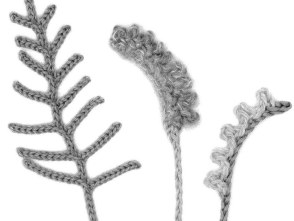

8

I've used...

+ **Yarn A:** Drops Muskat DK cotton
+ **Yarn B:** Drops Soft Tweed
+ 4mm (G/6) hook

Using Yarn A (Grey Blue), make a ch as long as desired for stem.

Row 1: 13 ch, skip 1 ch, slst in 1 ch, insert hook in next ch and pull Yarn B (Cream) through.

Row 2: (3 ch, slst in 3rd ch from hook, slst in 2 stem chs) 5 times.

Fasten off Yarn B and weave in ends.

9

I've used...

+ **Yarn A:** 1 strand Drops Brushed Alpaca Silk and 1 strand Wensleydale Longwool held together
+ **Yarn B:** Drops Muskat DK cotton
+ 4mm (G/6) hook

Using Yarn A (Grey/Blue Fluffy), make 11 ch.

Row 1: Skip 1 ch, dc in 10 ch, 1 ch, turn.

Row 2 (RS): Slst in 1 dc, (3 ch, skip 1 ch, slst in 2 ch, slst in next dc) 4 times, (2 ch, skip 1 ch, slst in 1 ch, slst in next dc) 5 times, 2 ch, slst in last dc. Fasten off.

Row 3: With RS facing, join Yarn B (Beige) with slst in 1 ch at base of seedhead, 1 dc in same st to secure. Work ch sts until stem is the desired length.

Fasten off and weave in ends.

10

I've used...

+ **Yarn A:** Drops Muskat DK cotton
+ **Yarn B:** Drops Safran 4-ply cotton
+ 3mm (D/3) and 4mm (G/6) hooks

Using Yarn A (Brown) and larger hook, make a magic ring.

Round 1 (RS): Slst, 2 ch (does not count as a st), 2 tr, 2 dtr, 2 tr, 2 ch, slst in ring. Fasten off Yarn A.

Round 2: With RS facing and smaller hook, join Yarn B (Yellow) with slst in first tr, (5 ch, skip 1 ch, 1 dc in 2 ch, 1 htr in 2 ch, slst in next st) 5 times.

Fasten off and weave in ends.

Terracotta Pot

This collage was inspired by the planting in an old weathered terracotta pot on my patio. It is filled with yellow and orange marigolds and trailing red geraniums, along with a variety of foliage. I wanted to explore using crochet stitches to create different leaf shapes. The tiny turquoise flowers provide a lovely cool counterpoint to the 'hot' colours of the other flowers...it is one of my own favourite colour combinations, but you could easily recreate this collage using your own favourite colour scheme.

6

9

8

4

2

1 *I've used...*

+ **Yarns A, B and C:** Drops Safran 4-ply cotton
+ 3.5mm (E/4) hook

Using Yarn A (Green), make a magic ring.

Round 1 (RS): 3 ch, 10 tr in ring, join with slst in top of 3-ch.

Round 2: 3 ch, 2 tr in each tr around, 2 ch, join with slst in first ch of beg 3-ch. Do not fasten off Yarn A, put a stitch marker in the working loop. (20 tr)

Round 3: Join Yarn B (Dark Red) with slst in 3ch-sp, 3 dc in same space, (1 dc in 1 tr, 2 dc in 1 tr) 10 times, [3 dc, slst] in 2ch-sp. Fasten off Yarn B.

Round 4: Using Yarn C (Light Green), and starting in 4th dc of Round 3, (slst in 1 dc, 1 dc in 1 dc, 2 htr in 1 dc) 10 times, slst in last dc worked into to finish. Fasten off Yarn C.

STEM

Remove stitch marker, put the working loop from Round 2 back on hook, 8 ch, skip 1 ch, slst in 7 ch, slst in beg 1 ch of Round 2.

Fasten off and weave in all ends.

 2 *I've used...*

+ **Yarns A and B:** Drops Safran 4-ply cotton
+ 3.5mm (E/4) hook

Using Yarn A (Dark Red), make a magic ring.

Round 1 (RS): 1 ch (counts as 1 dc), 9 dc in ring, join with slst in 1-ch, pulling Yarn B (Red) through.

Round 2: Continuing with Yarn B, 2 ch, [1 tr, 1 dtr, 1 tr] in 1 dc, 2 ch, slst in 1 dc, 4 ch, 1 dtr in 1 dc, 2 ch, slst in 1 dc, 4 ch, 1 dtr in 1 dc, 4 ch, slst in 1 dc, 2 ch, 1 dtr in 1 dc, 4 ch, slst in 1 dc, 2 ch, [1 tr, 1 dtr, 1 tr] in 1 dc, 2 ch, slst in slst from Round 1.

Fasten off Yarn B and weave in all ends.

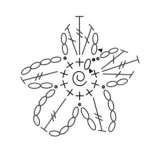

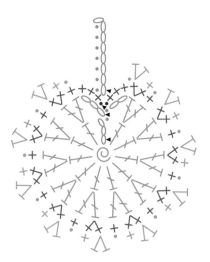

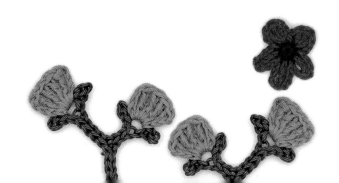

 3 *I've used...*

+ **Yarn A:** Scheepjes Catona 4-ply cotton
+ **Yarn B:** Drops Safran 4-ply cotton
+ 3.5mm (E/4) hook

STEM

Using Yarn A (Dark Green), make 11 ch, skip 1 ch, slst in 2 ch, 4 ch, skip 1 ch, slst in 2 ch, skip 1 ch (makes 1ch-sp to work first bud into), slst in 3 ch, 8 ch, skip 1 ch, slst in 2 ch, 4 ch, skip 1 ch, slst in 2 ch, skip 1 ch (makes 1ch-sp to work 2nd bud into), slst in remaining 10 stem chs.

BUDS

Using Yarn B (Peach), and working into the first 1ch-sp: [slst, 4 ch, 4 dtr, 4 ch, slst]. Fasten off.

Make another bud in the 2nd 1ch-sp.

Fasten off and weave in all ends.

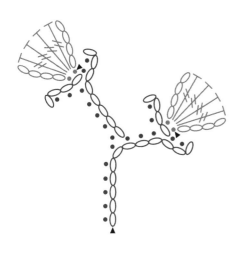

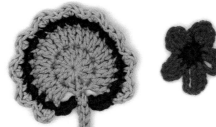

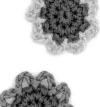

4 I've used...

+ **Yarn A:** Drops Safran 4-ply cotton
+ 3.5mm (E/4) hook

Using Yarn A (Green), make 10 ch for stem.

MAKE LEAF

Row 1 (RS): 5 ch, skip 3 ch, [1 tr, 1 ch, 1 tr] in 1 ch, 1 ch, turn.

Row 2: [1 dc in 1 tr, 1 dc in 1ch-sp] twice, 3 ch, turn.

Row 3: 1 tr in first dc, slst in 2 dc, 2 tr in 1 dc, 5 ch, slst in original 4th ch, slst in 1 ch.

Then [7 ch for stem, make leaf] twice, 4 ch for stem, make leaf, slst in 3 stem chs, make leaf, slst in 6 stem chs, make leaf, slst in 7 stem chs, make leaf, slst in remaining 13 stem chs.

Fasten off and weave in ends.

5 I've used...

+ **Yarn A:** Drops Muskat DK cotton
+ **Yarn B:** Drops Safran 4-ply cotton/Drops Alpaca
+ 3.5mm (E/4) hook

Using Yarn A (Orange), make a magic ring.

Round 1 (RS): 4 ch (counts as 1 tr, 1 ch), (1 tr, 1 ch) 6 times in ring, join with slst in 3rd ch of beg 4-ch, pulling through Yarn B (Yellow).

Round 2: Continuing with Yarn B, *[slst in 1ch-sp, 3 ch, 2tr-cl, 2 ch, skip 1 ch, slst in 1 ch, 3 ch, slst] in same 1ch-sp,** slst in 1 tr, repeat from * 5 times, and from * to ** once, slst in original slst at start of round to finish.

Fasten off and weave in ends.

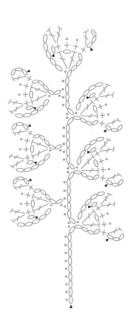

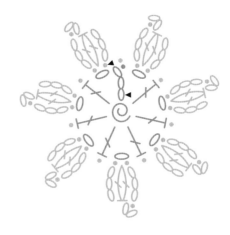

 6 *I've used...*

+ **Yarn A:** Drops Safran
  4-ply cotton
+ **Yarn B:** Drops Alpaca/
  Drops Safran 4-ply cotton
+ 3mm (D/3) hook

Using Yarn A (Brown), make a magic ring.

Round 1 (RS): 1 ch (counts as 1 dc), 8 dc in ring, join with slst in beg 1-ch. (9 dc)

Round 2: 1 ch (counts as 1 dc), 1 dc in same st, 2 dc in each dc around, join with slst in beg 1-ch, pulling Yarn B (Blue) through. (18 dc)

Round 3: Continuing with Yarn B, (4 ch, skip 1 dc, slst in next dc) 8 times, 4 ch, skip 1 dc, slst in slst from Round 2 to finish.

Fasten off and weave in ends.

 7 *I've used...*

+ **Yarn A:** Drops Flora (wool/
  alpaca blend)/Drops
  Safran 4-ply cotton
+ **Yarn B:** Drops Safran 4-ply
  cotton
+ 3.5mm (E/4) hook

Using Yarn A (Yellow), make 5 ch, slst in first ch to make a ring.

Round 1 (RS): 3 ch (counts as 1 tr), 11 tr in ring, slst in 3rd ch of beg 3 ch. (12 tr)

Round 2: 1 ch (counts as 1 dc), 1 dc in same st, 2 dc in each tr around, slst in 1 ch, pulling Yarn B (Orange) through.

Round 3: Continuing with Yarn B, [4 ch, 2 dtr in next 2 dc, 4 ch, slst in 1 dc] 7 times, 4 ch, 2 dtr in next 2 dc, 4 ch, slst in slst from Round 2.

Fasten off and weave in all ends.

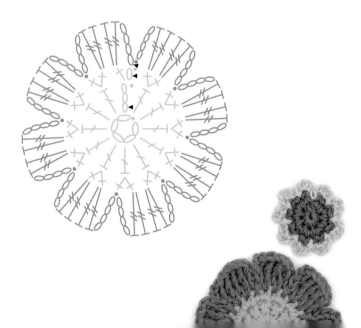

8

I've used...

+ **Yarn A:** Drops Safran 4-ply cotton
+ **Yarn B:** Drops Baby Alpaca Silk
+ 3mm (D/3) or 3.5mm (E/4) hook

STEM

Using Yarn A (Brown), work chs to give desired length of stem, skip 3 ch, slst in remaining stem chs. Fasten off Yarn A.

LEAF

With RS of stem facing, join Yarn B (Blue/Green) with slst in 3ch-sp at the end of the stem, (5 ch, skip 3 ch, 4tr-cl in 1 ch) 5 times, 3 ch, skip 2 ch, slst in 1 ch, working down the other side of the leaf, (4 ch, slst in the ch the 4tr-cl was worked into, slst in 1 ch) 5 times, slst in 3ch-sp.

Fasten off Yarn B and weave in all ends.

 9

I've used...

+ **Yarns A and B:** Drops Safran 4-ply cotton
+ 3.5mm (E/4) hook

Using Yarn A (Pale Yellow), make a magic ring.

Round 1 (RS): 1 ch (counts as 1 dc), 9 dc in ring, join with slst in beg 1-ch.

Round 2: 3 ch, 3 tr in 1 dc, 2 tr in 1 dc, 1 tr in 2 dc, [1 dtr, 1 ch, 1 dtr] in 1 dc, 1 tr in 2 dc, 2 tr in 1 dc, 3 tr in 1 dc, 3 ch, slst in slst from Round 1, pulling Yarn B (Dark Yellow) through.

Round 3: Continuing with Yarn B, 2 ch, 1 dc in 3rd of 3 ch, 2 dc in next 2 tr, 1 dc in 5 tr, 2 dc in 1 dtr, [1 dc, 2 ch, skip 1 ch, slst in 1 ch, 1 dc] in 1ch-sp, 2 dc in 1 dtr, 1 dc in 5 tr, 2 dc in next 2 tr, 1 dc in first of 3 ch, 2 ch, slst in beg slst.

STEM

Continuing with Yarn B, 9 ch, skip 1 ch, slst in 8 ch, slst in slst to finish.

Fasten off and weave in ends.

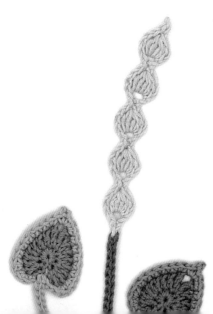

10 I've used...

+ **Yarns A and B:** Drops Safran 4-ply cotton
+ 3mm (D/3) hook

Using Yarn A (Pale Blue), make 5 ch, join with slst in first ch.

STEM (RS)

7 ch, skip 1 ch, slst in 6 ch, slst into ring, 5 dc in ring, 3 ch (counts as 1 tr), turn.

Row 1 (WS): 1 tr in 4 dc, 3 ch (counts as 1 tr), turn.

Row 2 (RS): 1 tr into same st, 2 tr in 1 tr, 2 dtr in 1 tr, 2 tr in 1 tr, 2 tr in top of 3-ch, 2 ch, turn.

Row 3: Skip first tr, 1 dc in 1 tr, 4 ch, skip 1 tr, 1 dc in 1 tr, 5 ch, skip 1 dtr, 1 dc in 1 dtr, 4 ch, skip 1 tr, 1 dc in 1 tr, 2 ch, skip 1 tr, slst in top of 3-ch. Fasten off Yarn A.

Row 4: With RS facing, join Yarn B (Blue) with slst in 2ch-sp, 2 dc in same space, slst in 1 dc, [1 htr, 1 tr, 1 ch, 1 tr, 1 htr] in 4ch-sp, slst in 1 dc, [1 htr, 1 tr, 1 dtr, 2 ch, skip 1 ch, slst in 1 ch, 1 dtr, 1 tr, 1 htr] in 5ch-sp, slst in 1 dc, [1 htr, 1 tr, 1 ch, 1 tr, 1 htr] in 4ch-sp, slst in 1 dc, [2 dc, slst] in 2ch-sp.

Fasten off Yarn B and weave in all ends.

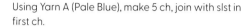

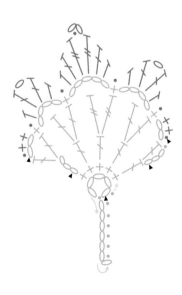

Poppy Posy

The idea for this arrangement started with a packet of wildflower seeds that I sowed one summer. I was delighted with the combination of red poppies, ox-eye daisies and cornflowers that sprang up. The bees, butterflies and hoverflies loved them! My garden is managed with wildlife and biodiversity at the forefront, and several areas of grass are always left uncut. As a result we get a lovely combination of wildflowers and the soft fluffy seedheads of the grasses. I have tried to recreate the effect with this collage.

The collage includes four stages in the poppy's life-cycle; the drooping, slightly hairy bud, the half-opened petals, a fully open flower and the brown seedhead.

The orange jug is based on an old, rather battered, enamel coffee pot that stands on a shelf in my kitchen, often filled with flowers picked from my garden.

1

9

8

10

I've used...
+ **Yarns A and B:** 4-ply cotton
+ 3.5mm (E/4) hook

Using Yarn A (Black), make a magic ring.

Round 1 (RS): 8 dc in ring, join with slst in FLO of first dc.

Round 2: (2 ch, slst in FLO of next dc) 7 times, 2 ch, slst in slst. Fasten off Yarn A.

Round 3: Join Yarn B (Red) with slst in BL of first dc from Round 1, (2 ch, skip 1 dc, slst in BLO of next dc) 3 times, 2 ch, slst in original BLO.

Round 4: Make petal: [slst, 5 ch, 9 trtr, 5 ch, slst] in first 2ch-sp, repeat in each 2ch-sp around (4 petals made).

Weave in all ends.

There is no need to block this design. To preserve the natural tendency of the petals to overlap and curl, I recommend spraying lightly with starch or stiffener after pulling the petals gently into place.

 I've used...
+ **Yarn A:** Drops Alpaca
+ **Yarn B:** 4-ply cotton
+ 3mm (D/3) hook

Using Yarn A (Yellow), make a magic ring.

Round 1 (RS): 3 ch (counts as 1 tr), 7 tr in ring, join with slst in FLO of 3rd ch, pulling Yarn B (White) through. Fasten off Yarn A, leaving a 20cm (8in) tail.

Round 2: Continuing with Yarn B, and working in FLO of the stitches of Round 1: (8 ch, slst in same st, slst in next tr) 8 times, fasten off invisibly (see Techniques: Crochet Stitches – Invisible Join).

Centre details: To make the yellow centre of the daisy pop up to give a 3D effect, thread the long tail of yellow yarn into a yarn needle, and with WS facing, thread it through the back loop of each treble crochet of Round 1, and pull gently to draw the stitches together.

Fasten off and weave in all ends.

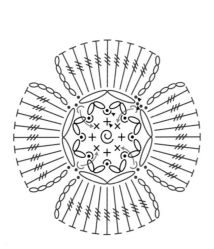

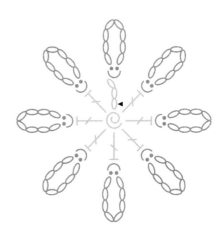

3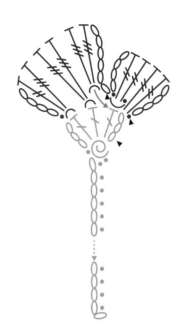

I've used...

+ **Yarn A:** 1 strand Drops Baby Alpaca Silk and 1 strand Drops Kid-Silk held together
+ **Yarn B:** Patons Cotton 4-ply
+ 3.5mm (E/4) hook

Using Yarn A (Blue/Green), make a magic ring.

Round 1 (RS): 3 ch (counts as 1 tr), 3 tr, 3 ch, slst in ring. Do not tighten magic ring. Work ch sts to make a stem of desired length, skip 1 ch, slst back along stem chs, slst in magic ring. Fasten off Yarn A and pull gently to tighten magic ring and close the centre.

Round 2: First petal: with RS facing, join Yarn B (Red) with slst in top of beg 3-ch. 4 ch, 2 dtr in same st, [2 dtr, 4 ch, slst] in FLO of next tr. To work the 2nd petal, hold the first petal forward, 1 ch, remove hook from working loop, insert hook from back to front under the back loop of the last tr worked into, put working loop back on hook and pull through, work 5 ch, 2 trtr into same back loop, 2 trtr in BLO of next tr, [1 trtr, 1 dtr, 4 ch, slst] in BLO of next tr.

Fasten off and weave in all ends.

Position the petals so that the front one curls slightly forwards, then spray with starch or stiffener to hold in place.

HELPFUL TIP

Any slightly fluffy yarn can be used for the stem and base of the half-opened poppy—it will recreate the soft delicate hairs on the stem.

I've used...

+ **Yarns A and B:** Drops Muskat DK cotton
+ 4mm (G/6) hook

STEM

Using Yarn A (Brown), ch number of stitches for desired length of stem, skip 3 ch, slst in remaining stem chs. Fasten off Yarn A.

SEEDHEAD

With RS of stem facing, join Yarn B (Beige) with slst in 3ch-sp at top of stem, 7 ch, skip 4 ch, 5tr-cl in 1 ch, 3 ch, skip 1 ch, slst in 2 ch, 2 ch, skip 1 ch, slst in 2 ch, 5 ch, slst in original ch that the 5tr-cl was worked into, slst in 2 ch, slst in 3ch-sp at top of stem.

Fasten off and weave in ends.

5

I've used...

+ **Yarns A, B and C:** Drops Muskat DK cotton
+ 4mm (G/6) hook

Using Yarn A (Green), make a magic ring.

Row 1 (WS): 2 ch, 4 tr in ring, 1 ch, turn. Pull yarn to tighten the magic ring, but do not close completely if you wish to attach a stem later.

Row 2 (RS): 1 dc in first tr, 2 dc in 3 tr. Fasten off Yarn A. (7 dc)

Row 3: With RS facing, and working in BLO of dc sts from Row 2, join Yarn B (Light Blue) with slst in first dc, 4 ch, slst in 1 dc, 5 ch, slst in 1 dc, ([6 ch, slst] in 1 dc) twice, 5 ch, slst in 1 dc, 4 ch, slst in 1 dc. Fasten off Yarn B.

Row 4: With RS facing, and working in FLO of dc sts from Row 2, join Yarn C (Dark Blue) with slst in 1 dc, ([3 ch, slst] in next dc) 6 times. Fasten off Yarn C.

To attach a stem, slst into the magic ring and ch sts to make a stem of desired length. Fasten off. Pull yarn to fully close the magic ring.

Weave in all ends.

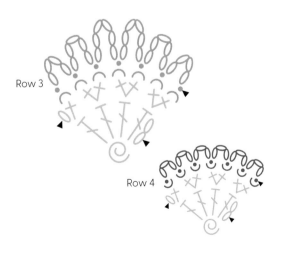

Row 3

Row 4

6

I've used...

+ **Yarn A:** Drops Alpaca
+ **Yarn B:** Drops Baby Alpaca Silk
+ 3mm (D/3) or 3.5mm (E/4) hook

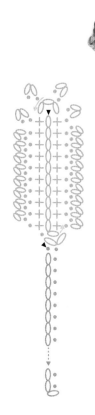

Round 1 (RS): Using Yarn A (Yellow), make 11 ch, skip 1 ch, dc in 10 ch, 3 ch, then continuing down the other side of the foundation ch, 1 dc in 10 ch, slst in 11th ch (turning ch).

Round 2: 2 ch, slst in first dc of Round 1, (2 ch, skip 1 ch, slst in 1 ch, slst in 1 dc) 9 times, (2 ch, skip 1 ch, slst in 1 ch, slst in 3ch-sp) twice, working back down the other side of the seedhead, (2 ch, skip 1 ch, slst in 1 ch, slst in next dc) 10 times. Fasten off Yarn A.

STEM

With RS facing, join Yarn B (Beige/Brown) with slst in 2ch-sp at the base of the seedhead, work chs to give length of stem required, skip 1 ch, slst in remaining stem chs, slst in 2ch-sp.

Fasten off and weave in all ends.

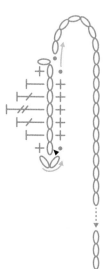

7

I've used...

+ **Yarn A:** 1 strand Drops Baby Alpaca Silk and 1 strand Drops Kid-Silk held together
+ 3.5mm (E/4) hook

Round 1 (RS): Using Yarn A (Blue Green), make 8 ch, skip 1 ch, [1 dc, 1 htr, 1 tr, 1 dtr, 1 tr, 1 htr, 1 dc] along 7 ch, 2 ch, working back along original 8 ch, slst in 1 ch, 1 dc in 5 ch, slst in 1 ch, slst in turning ch.

STEM

Work chs to give desired length of stem, fasten off.

Note: *The mohair yarn was chosen to achieve the slightly hairy texture of poppy buds and stems.*

Weave in all ends. When blocking, make sure the poppy bud is positioned to give a drooping effect.

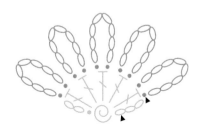

I've used...

+ **Yarn A:** Drops Baby Alpaca Silk
+ **Yarn B:** Fluffy yarn
+ 3.5mm (E/4) hook

Using Yarn A (Blue), make 5 ch, join with slst in first ch to make a ring.

Row 1 (RS): 4 ch (counts as 1 dtr), [2 tr, 2 ch, 2 tr, 1 dtr] in ring, 4 ch, turn.

Row 2: [2 tr, 2 ch, 2 tr] in 2ch-sp, skip 2 tr, 1 dtr in 4th of beg 4 ch, 4 ch, turn.

Row 3: [2 tr, 3 ch, 2 tr] in 2ch-sp, skip 2 tr, 1 dtr in top of beg 4-ch. Fasten off Yarn A.

LEAF EDGING

With RS facing, join Yarn B (Pale Blue/Grey) with slst in starting ring. 4 dc in 4ch-sp, 4 dc around 1 dtr on Row 2, [3 dc, 1 htr] in 4ch-sp on Row 3, [1 htr, 1 tr, 1 dtr, 2 ch, skip 1 ch, slst in 1 ch, 1 dtr, 1 tr, 1 htr] in 3ch-sp on Row 3, [1 htr, 3 dc] around 1 dtr on Row 3, 4 dc in 4ch-sp on Row 2, 4 dc around 1 dtr on Row 1, slst in starting ring. Fasten off Yarn B.

STEM

If you wish to add a stem, join yarn with a slst in the starting ring, work ch sts for desired length of stem.

Fasten off and weave in ends.

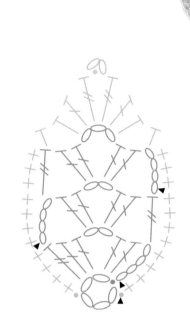

I've used...

+ **Yarn A:** Drops Alpaca
+ **Yarn B:** 4-ply cotton
+ 3mm (D/3) hook

Using Yarn A (Yellow), make a magic ring.

Row 1 (RS): [3 ch, 5 tr, 2 ch, slst] in ring. Fasten off Yarn A.

Row 2: With RS facing, and using Yarn B (White), work petals as follows: (slst in 1 tr, 8 ch, slst in same tr) 5 times.

Fasten off and weave in ends.

10 I've used...

+ **Yarn A:** Drops Muskat DK cotton
+ 4mm (G/6) hook

Using Yarn A (Orange), make 23 ch.

Row 1 (RS): Skip 3 ch, 1 tr in 20 ch, 3 ch (does not count as a st throughout), turn. (20 sts)

Row 2: Tr2tog, 1 tr in 16 tr, tr2tog, 3 ch, turn. (18 sts)

Row 3: Tr2tog, 1 tr in 14 tr, tr2tog, 3 ch, turn. (16 sts)

Row 4: 1 tr in 16 tr, 3 ch, turn.

Row 5: Tr2tog, 1 tr in 12 tr, tr2tog, 3 ch, turn. (14 sts)

Rows 6–8: 1 tr in 14 tr, 3 ch, turn.

Row 9: Tr2tog, 1 tr in 10 tr, tr2tog, 3 ch, turn. (12 sts)

Row 10: 1 tr in 12 tr, 3 ch, turn.

Row 11: 1 tr in 11 tr, 3 tr in 1 tr, 3 ch, turn. (14 sts)

Row 12: 2 tr in 2 tr, 1 tr in 12 tr, 3 ch, turn. (16 sts)

Row 13: 1 tr in 14 tr, 2 tr in 1 tr, [1 tr, 1 dtr] in 1 tr, 1 ch, turn. (18 sts)

Row 14: 1 dc in 1 dtr, 1 dc in 17 tr, 2 ch.

HANDLE

Row 15: 1 slst in 3ch-sp on Row 13, 1 slst around the end tr on Row 12, 14 ch, keeping RS facing, slst around the end tr on Row 8, slst in 3ch-sp on Row 7, 1 ch.

Row 16: 1 htr in 8 ch, 2 htr in next 3 ch, 1 htr in 3 ch, slst in slst at start of handle.

Fasten off and weave in ends.

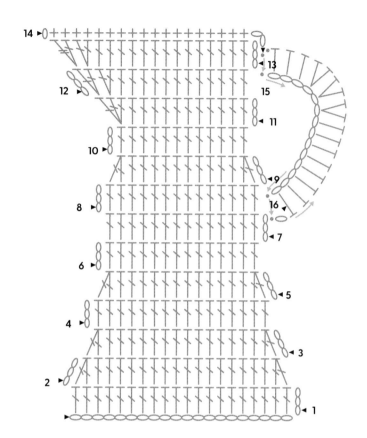

Autumn Wreath

As the seasons change, the pastel shades of summer gradually turn to the deeper, jewel-like colours of autumn. It's one of my favourite times of the year in the garden and is the inspiration behind this collage. There are still plenty of flowers around, with sunflowers and heleniums adding pops of gold, orange and bronze. We always have a bumper crop of shiny red crab apples, the rowan trees produce lots of tiny scarlet and orange berries, and small mushrooms and other fungi are often peeping up through the piles of fallen leaves beneath my sycamore tree.

For this collage, I've chosen thicker yarns in deep colours, to convey the richness of the season. Mercerised cotton yarn has a lovely sheen, perfect for leaves and berries. Tweedy yarn gives a different texture to some of the leaves and flowers, and the fluffy brushed alpaca yarn in the centres of the smaller flowers provides further contrasting texture.

I've used...

+ **Yarns A and B:** Drops Muskat DK cotton
+ 4mm (G/6) hook

Round 1 (RS): Using Yarn A (Orange), make 14 ch, skip 1 ch, slst in 13 ch, 1 ch.

Round 2: Working along the starting ch, slst in BL of first ch, skip 2 ch, 4 ch, 2tr-cl in BL of 1 ch, skip 2 ch, 4 ch, 2 dtr-cl in BLO of 1 ch, (skip 2 ch, 4 ch, 2tr-cl in BL of 1 ch) twice, 3 ch, 2tr-cl in turning ch from Round 1, 3 ch, working back down the other side, skip 1 slst, 2tr-cl in slst, skip 2 slsts, 4 ch, 2tr-cl in slst, skip 2 slsts, 4 ch, 2dtr-cl in slst, skip 2 slsts, 4 ch, 2tr-cl in slst, 4 ch, skip 2 slsts, slst in 1 ch at base of leaf.

STEM

7 ch, skip 1 ch, slst in 6 ch, slst in original ch at base of leaf to finish. Fasten off Yarn A.

Round 3: Join Yarn B (Brown) with slst in first 4ch-sp, *[1 dc, 1 htr, 1 tr, 1 htr, 1 dc]* into 4ch-sp, repeat from * in next three 4ch-sps, [1 dc, 2 htr, 1 tr] in 3ch-sp, 2 ch, [1 tr, 2 htr, 1 dc] in next 3ch-sp, repeat from * to * in remaining four 4ch-sps, slst in last 4ch-sp.

Fasten off Yarn B. Weave in all ends.

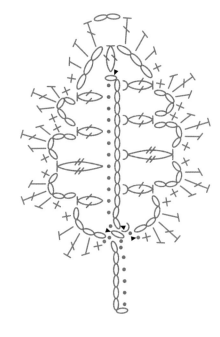

I've used...
+ **Yarn A:** Drops Muskat DK cotton
+ **Yarn B:** Drops Safran 4-ply cotton
+ 3mm (D/3) or 4mm (G/6) hook

APPLES (MAKE 3)

Using Yarn A (Red), make a magic ring.

Round 1 (RS): 1 ch (counts as 1 dc), 7 dc in ring, join with slst in beg 1-ch. (8 dc)

Round 2: 2 ch, [1 dc, 1 htr] in 1 dc, 2 htr in 5 dc, [1 htr, 1 dc] in 1 dc, join with slst in first of beg 2 ch. Fasten off and weave in ends.

STEM

Using Yarn B (Brown), make 10 ch, slst into 2ch-sp on RS of first apple, slst in 5 ch, 6 ch, slst into 2ch-sp on 2nd apple, slst in 6 ch, 4 ch, slst into 2ch-sp on 3rd apple, slst in remaining 9 stem chs.

Fasten off and weave in ends.

 I've used...
+ **Yarn A:** Drops Soft Tweed
+ **Yarn B:** Drops Alpaca
+ 4mm (G/6) hook

Round 1 (RS): Using Yarn A (Yellow), make 15 ch, skip 3 ch, 1 tr in 1 ch, (skip 2 ch, 2 ch, 1 tr in 1 ch) 3 times, 2 ch, skip 1 ch, slst in beg ch.

Round 2: 1 ch, [2 dc, 1 htr] in 2ch-sp, (3 tr in 2ch-sp) 3 times, [2 tr, 3 ch, 2 tr] in the end 3ch-sp, (3 tr in 2ch-sp) 3 times, [1 htr, 2 dc] in 2ch-sp, slst in beg 1 ch, pulling Yarn B (Mustard) through.

Round 3: Continuing with Yarn B, 1 ch, 1 dc in next 2 dc, 1 dc in 1 htr, 1 dc in 11 tr, [2 htr, 1 tr, 2 ch, skip 1 ch, slst in 1 ch, 1 tr, 2 htr] in 3ch-sp, 1 dc in 11 tr, 1 dc in 1 htr, 1 dc in next 2 dc, slst in beg 1 ch.

STEM

8 ch, skip 1 ch, slst in 7 ch, slst in 1 ch at base of leaf.

Fasten off and weave in ends.

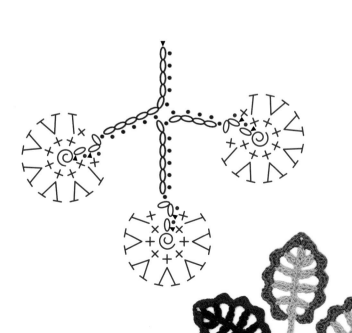

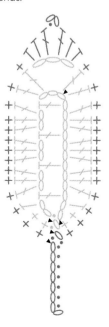

4   *I've used...*

+ **Yarn A:** Drops Soft Tweed
+ **Yarn B:** 1 strand Drops Baby Alpaca Silk and 1 strand Drops Kid-Silk held together
+ Oddments of 4-ply cotton or embroidery cotton for the French knots
+ 4mm (G/6) hook

OUTER PETALS

Using Yarn A (Dark Pink), make a magic ring.

Round 1: 10 dc in ring. (10 sts)

Round 2: Working in the BLO of the dc sts from Round 1, ([slst, 3 ch, 1 dtr] in 1 dc, [1 dtr, 3 ch, slst] in 1 dc) 5 times. Fasten off Yarn A.

INNER PETALS

Round 3: Using Yarn B (Lilac), and starting in FLO of first dc from Round 1, ([slst, 2 ch, 1 tr] in 1 dc, [1 tr, 2 ch, slst] in 1 dc) 5 times. Fasten off Yarn B.

CENTRE DETAILS

Using 4-ply cotton or embroidery cotton, work a French knot at the base of each inner petal.

Weave in all ends.

5 *I've used...*

+ **Yarns A and B:** Drops Muskat DK cotton
+ 4mm (G/6) hook

Using Yarn A (Beige), make 5 ch, slst in first ch to make a ring.

Round 1: [3 ch, 5 tr, 3 ch, slst] in ring.

Round 2: 1 ch, [slst, 2 dc, 2 ch, 1 dc] in 3ch-sp, 1 dc in 1 tr, [1 htr, 1 tr] in 1 tr, [1 dtr, 1 trtr, 1 dtr] in 1 tr, [1 tr, 1 htr] in 1 tr, 1 dc in 1 tr, [1 dc, 2 ch, 2 dc] in 3ch-sp, slst in 1 ch, pulling Yarn B (White) through.

STEM

Continuing with Yarn B, 10 ch, skip 2 ch, 1 htr in next 4 ch, 1 dc in next 4 ch, slst in original 1 ch at base of mushroom.

Fasten off and weave in ends.

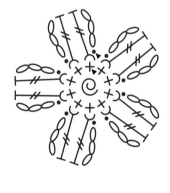

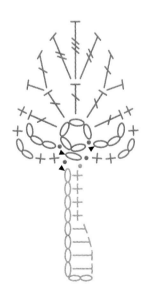

 6 *I've used...*

+ **Yarns A and B:** Drops Muskat DK cotton
+ 4mm (G/6) hook

 7 *I've used...*

+ **Yarn A :** Drops Muskat DK cotton
+ 4mm (G/6) hook

BERRIES

Using Yarn A (Orange), make 1 ch, (4 ch, skip 2 ch, 4tr-pc in 1 ch, 3 ch, slst in ch at base of popcorn, slst in 1 ch) 4 times, slst in beg 1-ch, pulling Yarn B (Brown) through.

STEM

Continuing with Yarn B, 7 ch, skip 1 ch, slst in 6 ch, slst in original 1 ch at base of berry cluster.

Fasten off and weave in ends.

Using Yarn A (Dark Red), make 5 ch, slst in first ch to make a ring.

Round 1 (RS): 6 ch, 1 dtr in ring, 4 ch, 1 dtr in ring, (6 ch, 1 dtr in ring) 4 times, 4 ch, 1 dtr in ring, 4 ch, join with slst in 2nd ch of beg 6-ch.

Round 2: 1 ch, [*1 dc, 1 htr, 1 tr, 2 ch, skip 1 ch, slst in 1 ch, 1 tr, 1 htr, 1 dc*] in the first two 4ch-sps, [1 dc, 1 htr, 1 tr, 1 dtr, 2 ch, skip 1 ch, slst in 1 ch, 1 dtr, 1 tr, 1 htr, 1 dc] in first 6ch-sp, [1 dc, 2 htr, 2 tr, 2 dtr, 2 ch, skip 1 ch, slst in 1 ch] in 2nd 6ch-sp, [2 dtr, 2 tr, 2 htr, 1 dc] in 3rd 6ch-sp, [1 dc, 1 htr, 1 tr, 1 dtr, 2 ch, skip 1 ch, slst in 1 ch, 1 dtr, 1 tr, 1 htr, 1 dc] in 4th 6ch-sp, repeat from * to * in the final two 4ch-sps, slst in beg 1-ch.

STEM

8 ch, skip 1 ch, slst in 7 ch, slst in beg 1 ch.

Fasten off and weave in ends.

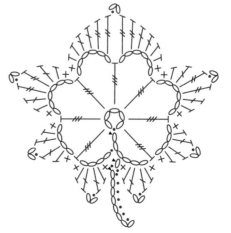

8 *I've used...*

- **Yarns A and B:** Drops Muskat DK cotton

- 4mm (G/6) hook

STEM

Using Yarn A (Brown), make 20 ch, skip 3 ch, slst in next 3 ch, 9 ch, skip 3 ch, slst in next 4 ch, 7 ch, skip 3 ch, slst in remaining 20 stem chs. Fasten off Yarn A.

FLOWERS

Join Yarn B (Orange) with slst in the first 4ch-sp, (7 ch, skip 3 ch, 1 tr in 1 ch, 1 htr in 1 ch, 1 dc in next 2 ch, slst in ring) 3 times. Fasten off. Work a flower into the 2nd 4ch-sp in the same way.

BUDS

Join Yarn B with slst in the 3rd 4ch-sp, (4 ch, skip 2 ch, 1 htr in 1 ch, 1 dc in 1 ch, slst in ring) twice.

Fasten off and weave in all ends.

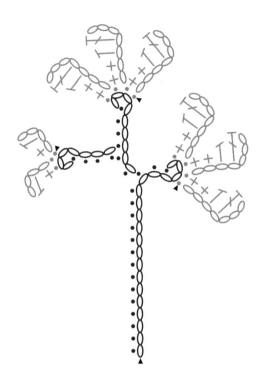

Helpful Tip

The flowers and bud in Motif 8 could be worked using a yarn with a gradual colour change, which would give a lovely natural effect.

 9 I've used…

+ **Yarn A:** Drops Muskat DK cotton
+ **Yarn B:** Drops Soft Tweed/ Drops Muskat DK cotton
+ 4mm (G/6) hook

Using Yarn A (Brown), make a magic ring.

Round 1 (RS): 1 ch (counts as 1 dc throughout), 6 dc in ring, join with slst in beg 1-ch. (7 sts)

Round 2: 1 ch, 1 dc in same stitch, 2 dc in each dc around, join with slst in beg 1-ch. (14 sts)

Round 3: 1 ch, 1 dc in 1 dc, (2 dc in 1 dc, 1 dc in 1 dc) 6 times, join with slst in beg 1-ch, pulling Yarn B (Yellow) through. (20 sts)

Round 4: Continuing with Yarn B, (*3 ch, 3tr-cl in 1 dc, 2 ch, skip 1 ch, slst in 1 ch, **slst in next dc) 9 times, repeat from * to ** once more, fasten off invisibly (see Techniques: Crochet Stitches – Invisible Join).

 10 I've used…

+ **Yarn A:** Drops Safran 4-ply cotton/Drops Alpaca
+ 3mm (D/3) hook

Using Yarn A (Lime Green), make 10 ch for stem (can be varied).

Make leaf: [6 ch, skip 1 ch, slst in 1 ch, 1 dc in 1 ch, 1 htr in 1 ch, 1 dc in 1 ch, slst in 1 ch].

(3 ch, make leaf) 3 times, (make leaf, slst in 3 ch) 4 times, slst in remaining stem chs.

Fasten off and weave in ends.

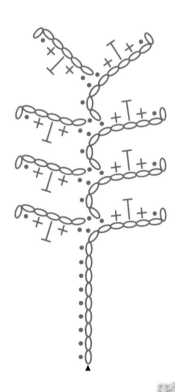

Midwinter Magic

This collage is a bouquet to celebrate the magic of the winter season. Although many plants die back during the colder months, there is still plenty of interest to be found, including evergreen conifers, fluffy dried seedheads and berries. I wanted to highlight the contrasting shapes of the foliage.

I often discover leaves that have partially decomposed, revealing the skeleton of veins behind. The filigree patterns are incredibly intricate and are especially beautiful on frosty mornings. I've tried to recreate this effect using metallic yarns and embroidery threads to add silvery, frost-dusted edges to some of the foliage. Further inspiration came from dew-speckled cobwebs strung across the garden paths and hedges.

I chose deep rich reds and corals for the flowers both to complement the berries and also to contrast with the colour palette of the garden during its winter sleep.

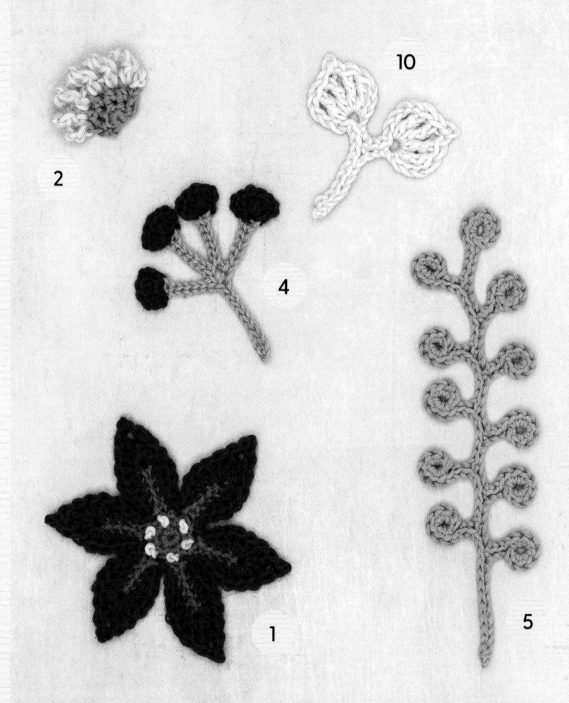

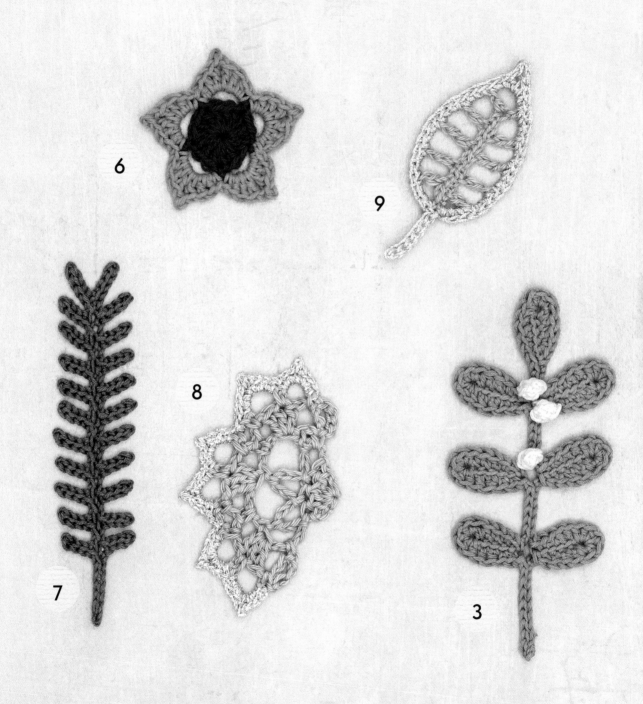

6

9

8

7

3

1

I've used...

+ **Yarns A and B:** Drops Flora (wool/alpaca blend)
+ Oddments of contrasting DK cotton yarn for French knots
+ 3.5mm (E/4) hook

Using Yarn A (Coral), make 4 ch, join with slst to form a ring.

Round 1 (RS): 1 ch (counts as 1 dc throughout), 5 dc in ring, join with slst in beg 1-ch. (6 sts)

Round 2: 1 ch, 1 dc in same st, 2 dc in each dc around, join with slst in beg 1-ch. (12 sts)

Round 3: (*8 ch, skip 3 ch, slst in next 5 ch, 1 ch, skip 1 dc*, slst in 1 dc)] 5 times, repeat from * to * once more, slst in slst from Round 2 to finish. Fasten off Yarn A.

Round 4: Join Yarn B (Red) with slst in first 1ch-sp between first and second petals, (slst in 1 ch, 1 dc in 1 ch, 1 htr in 1 ch, 1 tr in next 2 ch, [2 tr, 1 dtr, 2 ch, skip 1 ch, slst in 1 ch, 1 dtr, 2 tr] in 3ch-sp, 1 tr in next 2 slst, 1 htr in 1 slst, 1 dc in 1 slst, slst in 1ch-sp) 6 times. Fasten off Yarn B.

Details: Using the contrasting DK cotton yarn, work a French knot near the base of each petal.

Fasten off and weave in all ends.

2

I've used...

+ **Yarn A:** Drops Safran 4-ply cotton
+ **Yarn B:** 1 strand of 4-ply cotton and 1 strand Drops Brushed Alpaca Silk held together
+ 3.5mm (E/4) hook

Using Yarn A (Blue Green), make a magic ring.

Row 1 (RS): 2 ch (does not count as st), 5 htr in ring, 2 ch, turn. (5 htr)

Row 2: 1 htr in 5 htr, pull Yarn B (Pale Blue) through on final stitch, turn.

Row 3: Continuing with Yarn B, 3 ch, 1 trtr in same stitch, 1 trtr in next 3 htr, [1 trtr, 3 ch, slst] in last htr.

Fasten off and weave in ends.

The long stitches will curl over to make the petals.

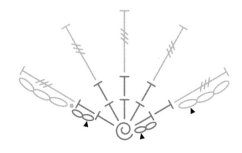

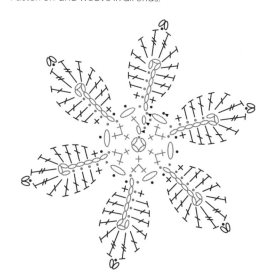

3

I've used...

+ **Yarns A and B:** Drops Safran 4-ply cotton
+ 3mm (D/3) and 3.5mm (E/4) hooks

STEM

Using Yarn A (Green) and larger hook, make 9 ch.

MAKE LEAF

Round 1 (RS): 9 ch, skip 3 ch, slst in next 6 ch, pass yarn under work.

Round 2: Slst in 1 ch, 1 dc in next 2 ch, 1 htr in next 2 ch, 5 htr in 3ch-sp, 1 htr in BLO of next 2 slsts, 1 dc in BLO of next 2 slsts, slst in BLO of slst.

(6 ch for stem, make leaf) twice more, 3 ch for stem, make leaf, slst in 3 stem chs, make leaf, (slst in 6 stem chs, make leaf) twice, slst in remaining 9 stem chs.

BERRIES

Using the smaller hook, join Yarn B (Cream) with slst in the space between two opposite leaves, 2 ch, skip 1 ch, 4tr-pc in 1 ch, 2 ch, slst into same 1 ch as popcorn, slst into space between leaves once more. Fasten off.

Place more berries as desired.

Fasten off and weave in ends.

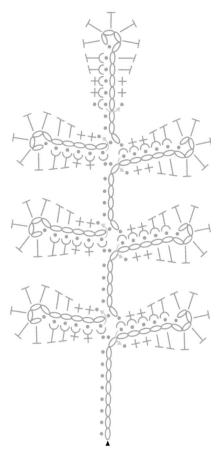

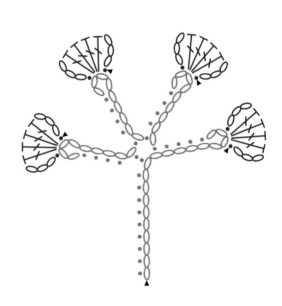

4 I've used...

+ **Yarn A:** Drops Baby Alpaca Silk
+ **Yarn B:** Drops Flora (wool/alpaca blend)
+ 3mm (D/3) hook

STEM

Using Yarn A (Beige), make 10 ch for main stem, (9 ch, skip 4 ch, slst in next 5 ch) 4 times, slst in 10 stem chs. Fasten off Yarn A.

BERRIES

Using Yarn B (Red), [slst, 3 ch, 4 tr, 3 ch, slst] in the 3ch-sp at the end of the first stem.

Make another berry in each 3ch-sp.

Fasten off Yarn B and weave in all ends.

HELPFUL TIP

When sewing in yarn ends, pull both ends through to the back of the berry, thread both at the same time into your yarn needle, work a couple of back stitches through the back of the treble crochet stitches then fasten off.

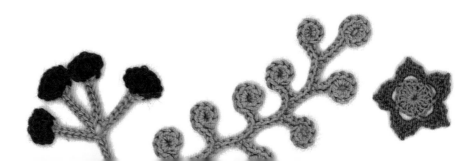

5 *I've used...*

+ **Yarn A:** Drops Safran 4-ply cotton
+ 3.5mm (E/4) hook

Using Yarn A (Green), make 10 ch for stem,

Make leaf: [6 ch, skip 2 ch, slst in 1 ch, pass yarn under work, 8 dc in 3ch-sp, slst in next 3 ch].

(5 ch for stem, make leaf) 5 more times, working back down the other side of the stem, slst in 2 stem chs, (make leaf, slst in 5 stem chs) 5 times, slst in remaining stem chs.

Fasten off and weave in ends.

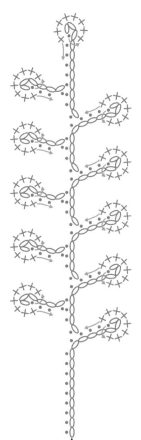

6 *I've used...*

+ **Yarns A and B:** Drops Safran 4-ply cotton/Drops Flora (wool/alpaca blend)
+ 3.5mm (E/4) hook

Using Yarn A (Red), make 5 ch, join with slst in first ch to make a ring.

Round 1 (RS): 3 ch (counts as 1 tr), 14 tr in ring, join with slst in top of 3-ch. (15 tr)

Round 2: (5 ch, skip next 2 tr, slst in 1 tr) 4 times, 5 ch, slst in slst from Round 1, pulling Yarn B (Coral) through.

Round 3: Continuing with Yarn B, ([1 dc, 1 htr, 2 tr, 2 ch, skip 1 ch, slst in 1 ch, 2 tr, 1 htr, 1 dc] in 5ch-sp, sl st in sl st) 5 times.

Fasten off and weave in ends.

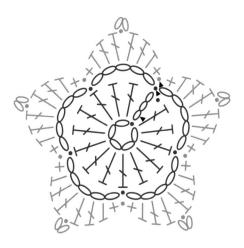

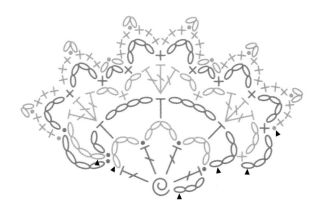

7

I've used...

+ **Yarn A:** Drops Safran 4-ply cotton
+ 3.5mm (E/4) hook

Using Yarn A (Turquoise), make 6 ch for stem.

Fronds: (5 ch, skip 1 ch, slst in next 4 ch, 1 ch for stem) 10 times, (5 ch, skip 1 ch, slst in next 4 ch) twice, (slst in 1 ch of stem, 5 ch, skip 1 ch, slst in 4 ch) 10 times, slst in remaining 6 stem chs.

Fasten off and weave in ends.

8

I've used...

+ **Yarn A:** Scheepjes Catona 4-ply cotton
+ **Yarn B:** Metallic yarn such as DMC Lumina/ Anchor Artiste Metallic/Lammy Lurex
+ 3mm (D/3) and 3.5mm (E/4) hooks

Using Yarn A (Pale Grey) and larger hook, make a magic ring.

Row 1 (WS): 3 ch (does not count as st), 4 tr in ring, 4 ch, turn.

Row 2 (RS): Skip first tr, slst in 1 tr, (4 ch, slst in 1 tr) twice, 4 ch, turn.

Row 3: (1 htr in 4ch-sp, 4 ch) twice, [1 htr, 2 ch, slst] in 4ch-sp, 4 ch, turn.

Row 4: (3 tr in 1 htr, [2 ch, 1 dc, 2 ch] in 4ch-sp) twice, 3 tr in 1 htr, [3 ch, 1 dc] in 4ch-sp, 4 ch, turn.

Row 5: 1 dc in 3ch-sp, (4 ch, skip 1 tr, 1 dc in 1 tr, 4 ch, 1 dc in 2ch-sp, 2 ch, 1 dc in next 2ch-sp) twice, 4 ch, skip 1 tr, 1 dc in 1 tr, 4 ch, slst in 4ch-sp, 4 ch, slst in slst at end of Row 3. Fasten off Yarn A.

Row 6: With RS facing and using smaller hook, join Yarn B (Silver) with slst in first dc from Row 5, ((*[3 dc, 2 ch, skip 1 ch, slst in 1 ch, 3 dc] in 4ch-sp) twice*, 1 ch, slst in 2ch-sp, 1 ch) twice, work from * to * once more, finish with slst in slst.

Fasten off and weave in ends.

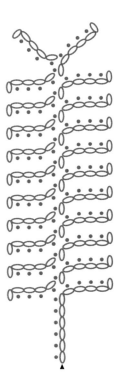

9

I've used...

+ **Yarn A:** Drops Baby Alpaca Silk
+ **Yarn B:** DMC Metallic Silver embroidery thread
+ 3mm (D/3) hook

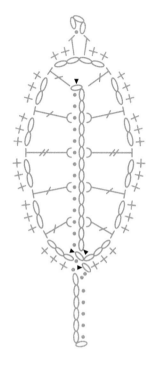

Using Yarn A (Blue), make 15 ch, skip 1 ch, slst in 14 ch.

Round 1: 4 ch, (skip 2 ch, 1 tr in BLO of 1 ch, 2 ch) twice, skip 2 ch, 1 dtr in BLO of 1 ch, 2 ch, skip 2 ch, 1 tr in BLO of 1 ch, 2 ch, skip 2 ch, [1 tr, 4 ch, 1 tr] in turning ch, 2 ch, skip 2 slsts, 1 tr in BLO of 1 slst, 2 ch, skip 2 slsts, 1 dtr in BLO of 1 slst, 2 ch, skip 2 slsts, 1 tr in BLO of 1 slst, 2 ch, skip 2 slsts, 1 tr in BLO of 1 slst, 3 ch, slst in first of beg 4-ch pulling through Yarn B (Silver).

Round 2: Continuing with Yarn B, 1 ch, 3 dc in 4ch-sp, (3 dc in 2ch-sp) 4 times, [2 dc, 1 htr, 3 ch, skip 2 ch, slst in 1 ch, 1 htr, 2 dc] in 4ch-sp, (3 dc in 2ch-sp) 4 times, 3 dc in 3ch-sp, slst in beg 1-ch.

STEM

7 ch, skip 1 ch, slst in 6 ch, slst in 1 ch at base of leaf.

Fasten off and weave in ends.

10

I've used...

+ **Yarn A:** Drops Muskat DK cotton
+ 4mm (G/6) hook

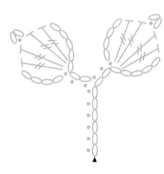

Using Yarn A (Pale Coral), make 6 ch for stem.

Make leaf: [7 ch, skip 4 ch, [2 dtr, 2 ch, skip 1 ch, slst in 1 ch, 2 dtr, 4 ch, slst] in 1 ch, slst in next 2 ch].

Make leaf, slst in 6 stem chs.

Fasten off and weave in ends.

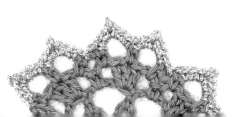

Techniques

GENERAL INFORMATION

ABBREVIATIONS

beg: beginning

BL: back loop

BLO: work into the back loop only

ch(s): chain(s)

ch sp: chain space

dc: double crochet

dc2tog: double crochet 2 stitches together

dtr: double treble crochet

FLO: work into the front loop only

htr: half treble crochet

RS: right side

slst(s): slip stitch(es)

sp: space

st(s): stitch(es)

tr: treble crochet

tr2tog: treble crochet 2 stitches together

trtr: triple treble crochet

WS: wrong side

yrh: yarn round hook

2(3,4,5)tr-cl: 2(3,4,5) treble cluster

2(4)dtr-cl: 2(4) double treble cluster

3(4)tr-pc: 3(4) treble popcorn

4dtr-pc: 4 double treble popcorn

TERMINOLOGY

All the patterns in this book are written using UK crochet terms. See the table below for the equivalent US stitch names.

UK TERM	US TERM
double crochet	single crochet
treble crochet	double crochet
half treble crochet	half double crochet
double treble crochet	treble crochet
triple treble crochet	double treble crochet
yarn round hook	yarn over hook

SYMBOL KEY

Here's a guide to the symbols used in the charts:

ℂ magic ring	2tr-cl
◯ chain	3tr-cl
● slip stitch	4tr-cl
+ double crochet	5tr-cl
◄ start	2dtr-cl
∩ back loop only	4dtr-cl
∪ front loop only	3tr-pc
T half treble crochet	4tr-pc
T treble crochet	4dtr-pc
T double treble crochet	treble 2 together
T triple treble crochet	

CROCHET STITCHES

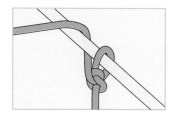

CHAIN

Start with a slip knot on the hook. Wrap yarn round hook. Pull hook through the loop of the slip knot to make one chain stitch.

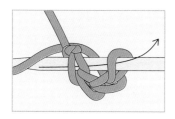

SLIP STITCH

Insert hook into a stitch, wrap yarn round hook and pull loop through the stitch and the loop on the hook.

MAGIC RING

With the tail end of the yarn hanging down, make a loop and hold it securely between two fingers. Insert the hook in the loop and pull the yarn through [1], make a chain stitch to secure, and begin making stitches inside the loop [2]. When you have finished pull the tail to tighten the loop [3]. Slip stitch in the first stitch to join.

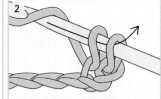

DOUBLE CROCHET

Insert hook through stitch, wrap yarn round hook (yrh), pull through the stitch [1] (2 loops on hook), yrh and pull through both loops on hook [2] (one loop remaining on hook).

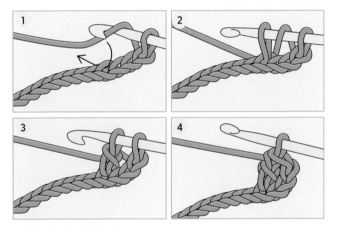

TREBLE CROCHET

Wrap yarn round hook (yrh) and insert hook in stitch [1]. Yrh and pull through the stitch [2]. Yrh, pull through 2 loops (2 loops on hook) [3]. Yrh again, and pull through 2 loops (1 loop left on hook) [4].

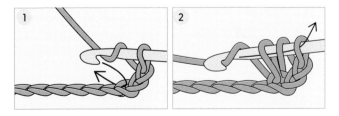

HALF TREBLE CROCHET

Yarn round hook (yrh), insert hook in stitch [1], yrh and pull through the stitch (3 loops on hook). Yrh once more, pull through all 3 loops [2] (1 loop remaining on hook).

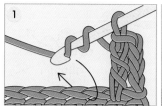

DOUBLE TREBLE CROCHET

Wrap yarn round hook (yrh) twice [1], insert hook in stitch, yrh and pull through the stitch. Yrh and pull through 2 loops [2] (3 loops left on hook). Yrh and pull through 2 loops (2 loops left on hook). Yrh and pull through 2 loops (1 loop remaining on hook).

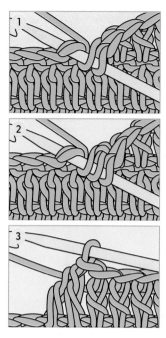

TR2TOG

Yrh, insert hook in stitch [1], yrh, pull through stitch, yrh, pull through 2 loops (2 loops left on hook). Yrh, insert hook in next stitch [2], yrh, pull through 2 loops, yrh, pull through remaining 3 loops on hook [3].

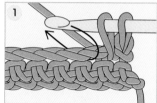

DC2TOG

Insert hook in stitch, yrh and pull through (2 loops on hook) [1]. Insert hook in next stitch, yrh, and pull through (3 loops on hook). Yrh again, and pull through all 3 loops on hook [2] (1 loop left on hook).

TRIPLE TREBLE CROCHET

This is worked similarly to a double treble crochet, but you'll wrap the yarn round the hook 3 times instead of 2 to start. Wrap yarn round hook (yrh) 3 times, insert hook into stitch, yrh and pull through the stitch. Yrh, pull through 2 loops (4 loops left on hook). Yrh, pull through 2 loops (3 loops left on hook). Yrh and pull through 2 loops (2 loops left on hook). Yrh and pull through last 2 loops (1 loop remaining on hook).

POPCORN STITCH

Work 4 tr (can vary) into same stitch, remove hook from working loop and insert it into top of first treble in the group. Insert hook back into working loop and pull it through top of first treble [1 and 2].

CLUSTER STITCHES

Work first stitch given up to last pull through [1], repeat for remaining number of stitches required in same stitch, then yarn round hook and pull through all loops on hook [2].

 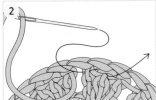

INVISIBLE JOIN

After working the last stitch of the round, cut yarn leaving a 20cm (8in) tail, and pull this through. Thread onto a yarn needle, pass needle from front to back through the top 2 loops of the first stitch of the round, then from front to back under the back loop of the final stitch [1]. Pull through so the stitch is the same tension as the rest of the stitches, and you will have created an almost invisible join. Weave in the yarn tail at the back of the work as usual [2].

EMBROIDERY STITCHES

Use a selection of these simple embroidery stitches to put extra details on your flowers or leaves, or add some pretty decoration to a crocheted bowl or vase.

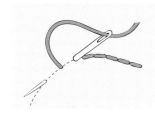

BACK STITCH

Bring needle up from back of work, make a small stitch backwards. Bring needle up again a little way in front of first stitch. Re-insert needle where first stitch ended. Repeat until you have the desired length of stitches. Ideal for stems.

STRAIGHT STITCH

Bring needle up from back of work, then re-insert where desired to form a single straight stitch. Vary the length and angle to create different effects. A great stitch for adding detail to flower centres.

FRENCH KNOTS

Bring needle up from back of work, wrap yarn around the needle two or three times, then, keeping yarn taut with your other hand, re-insert needle back into the fabric, close to where it came up. Pull until the yarn disappears and a knot forms.

CHAIN STITCH

Bring needle up from back of work, hold the yarn away to form a loop. Re-insert needle in same hole and bring the point up through the fabric again a short distance away. Pull the yarn through, making sure the working yarn is under the needle.

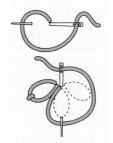

LAZY DAISY STITCH

Work a single chain stitch, then anchor the loop with a small straight stitch. Work several stitches in a circle to form a 'lazy daisy' flower. Alter the shape of the petals by working longer or shorter chain stitches.

OTHER TECHNIQUES

This section provides some useful tips for finishing off your crocheted pieces to make them really look their best before you apply them to your chosen project

SIMPLE STEMS

Some of the motifs have stem instructions included as part of the pattern. However, others just have the flower on its own, and you may wish to attach a stem. Of course, the length you need will vary depending on your own project, but the basic method is the same.

MAKING THE STEM

Simply make a chain which is the length you need for your stem, skip 1 chain, then slip stitch back along the length of the chain. If you would like a slightly more substantial stem, then instead of slip stitching back along the chain, you can use double crochet stitches. If you require a thinner, more delicate, stem, simply work a chain of the appropriate length without slip stitching back along. You can also vary the thickness and texture of the stems by choosing yarns made from different fibres.

ATTACHING THE FLOWER TO THE STEM

There are several ways to attach your flower to a stem:

+ You can add it as you work your stem. Once you've got a chain the length you need for your stem, slip stitch into the back of your flower (perhaps behind one of the central stitches, or somewhere near the base of a petal), then skip 1 chain, and slip stitch back along your stem.

+ Make the stem separately, then attach your flower with a couple of small stitches using a sewing needle and thread. Alternatively, you can leave a long tail of yarn when you complete the flower, and use this to stitch the flower to the stem.

+ Make the stem separately, and use a small dab of PVA glue to fix the stem in position behind your flower. This method is excellent if you are creating something like a picture, but bear in mind that if the item you're attaching the flowers to might need washing, for example a cushion cover or an item of clothing, then this is not a suitable method to use.

BLOCKING AND STIFFENING

Most of the patterns in this book benefit from being blocked. Blocking improves the shape and definition of the pieces, and is very easy to do. You don't need any special equipment. I use an old towel, folded over, and some pins. Pin out the motif so that it is slightly stretched, paying particular attention to the points of the leaves or petals. At picot points, put the pin in the skipped stitch(es) and stretch it out a little. I like to use a spray starch, or stiffener, to give some stability to the pieces. However, plain water sprayed on and left to dry will also help the piece stay in shape if you prefer to keep it simple. Longer stems in particular have a tendency to twist and curl. To help counteract this, I often give them a second spray of starch or stiffener once the first coat has dried.

MAKING MOTIFS 3D

If you prefer your flower petals to be more three-dimensional, or your leaves to slightly curl, you can encourage them into the desired position with your fingers, then spray them liberally with starch or stiffener before leaving to air dry. A second coat will provide extra stability. A firmer effect may be obtained by soaking the item in a liquid starch, before coaxing into shape and leaving to dry. Bear in mind, however, that any item which becomes damp, or is washed, will lose its stiffness and will require re-starching.

HELPFUL TIPS

SEWING IN MULTIPLE YARN TAILS

When adding lots of little flowers or buds to a stem, it's inevitable that there will be a lot of yarn ends to deal with. I find it saves a little time and effort if they can be dealt with two at a time. Make sure both ends are close together, for example, on the same small bud, then pull them both through to the back of the work. Trim them to the same length, then thread both at the same time into your yarn needle and sew in as usual.

USING VARIEGATED YARNS FOR A MORE NATURAL EFFECT

Flowers naturally have subtle variations in colour, and choosing a yarn with a long colour change enables you to achieve this with the crocheted motifs. If you make several flowers with the same variegated yarn, they will all be a slightly different shade, and this gives a lovely natural effect when they are placed together in a collage.

ADDING DIFFERENT TEXTURES

I've used a few additional elements to style my collages, such as fabrics with different textures, old lace, vintage embroidered linens and pieces of driftwood salvaged from seaside holidays. I would suggest if you're planning to make your motifs into a picture or to add them to a textile art piece, it's a good idea to start collecting a few extra items together, to add depth, detail and structure to your design.

MORE INSPIRATION

Although most of my creative inspiration comes from my garden, I also find I pick up ideas for arranging motifs and creating collages from lots of other, sometimes quite unexpected, places.

SOURCES OF INSPIRATION

The way you use or combine the motifs will be a very personal choice, and may be very different from the collages I've presented in this book. Here are a few suggestions for places to look for ideas to use when creating your own arrangements. Inspiration can be found everywhere! The natural world is full of possibilities... whether it's a few wildflowers you notice when you're out for a walk, or the beautiful colours of foliage as the seasons change.

Away from nature, I often discover pleasing colour schemes, floral arrangements and designs on artworks or decorative ceramics, which might inspire the way I arrange my motifs in a collage. Beautiful floral embroidery can also be an influence. Even things like wallpaper, gift wrap, colourful printed fabrics and pretty stationery can be a source of creative inspiration! So the next time you're out for a ramble in the countryside, or a browse around the shops, art galleries or vintage markets, take a few photographs or make some notes!

IDEAS FOR USING THE MOTIFS

I hope my collages will give you lots of
ideas and inspiration to create your own
crocheted pictures. You can replicate
each collage as given, or you may want
to transform my arrangements by making
the motifs in your own colour scheme. The
patterns can be combined in so many ways,
to give an endless variety of arrangements.
You can take elements from different
collages and put them together to make your
own, unique combinations of your favourite
flowers and foliage.

There are many ways to use this collection of
crochet motifs. You could make a seasonal
arrangement, and fix it in a box frame to
create a unique piece of yarn art, or use the
motifs to make a wall hanging in colours
to complement your décor. The designs
could be stitched onto a plain cushion
cover, a canvas shopping bag, or items of
clothing or hats. They could be used to make
beautiful greeting cards, or to add a unique
decorative touch to your gift-wrapping. I
love to spend time just 'playing' with my box
of flowers and leaves, creating an ephemeral
piece of art. It absorbs my mind completely
for a few moments, so it's a very mindful
activity, and very relaxing.

Whichever way you decide to use the motifs,
I hope you will have fun experimenting!

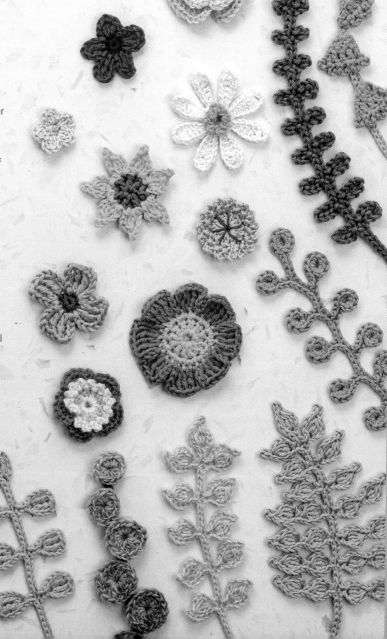

ABOUT THE AUTHOR

After completing her degree in Geography at Durham University, Chris taught in primary schools for several years. Having always had an interest in crafting, she started her own business called 'Chris made this' selling handmade gifts online and at craft fairs once her two children were grown up. She now focusses on creating her own crochet designs and sharing colourful crochet inspiration through her social media. Chris has designed and made crochet work that has been incorporated into various collections shown at London Fashion Week. As well as crochet and gardening, Chris enjoys walking, reading, knitting, photography and yoga, and lives in North Yorkshire with her husband.

If you are interested in seeing more of Chris's creative work and garden, she can be found on Instagram **@chris.made.this** and **@tales.from.north.end** and on Facebook as **Chris made this**.

ACKNOWLEDGEMENTS

Writing my first book has been an incredibly exciting adventure, and one which I've thoroughly enjoyed. I'm very grateful to have been given the opportunity, and would like to thank Sarah and all the team at David and Charles for all their help and support during the process.

Thanks to all of my family and friends for their encouragement and enthusiasm for my creative ventures, particularly my mum and dad, and my children Tom and Becky, for all their love and support. Becky, as an artist herself, has given endless encouragement and advice, and I must also thank her for making me the pot for the Terracotta Pot collage and for supplying some of her pretty artwork for the photograph at the beginning of the Techniques section. I couldn't have completed the book without the love and support of my husband Paul, who has given me the time and space to work, provided endless cups of coffee and excellent banana bread to keep me going, and hasn't complained when the house has seemed to be gradually filling up with crocheted flowers!

YARN SUPPLIERS

I bought, or already had, all of the yarns myself so didn't receive any yarn support from a company. My main supplier of Drops yarn was Purple Sheep Yarns based in Lancashire, via their website: **www.purplesheepyarns.co.uk**

Here are some other useful yarn suppliers:

Wool Warehouse: **www.woolwarehouse.co.uk**

Hedgerow Yarns: **www.hedgerowyarns.co.uk** (for hand-dyed sock yarn)

INDEX

apple blossom 24, 27, 31
Autumn Wreath (collage) 94–103

back stitch 121
berries 104, 106–7, 109–10
blocking 122
blossom 24, 27, 31

campanula 34, 37–8
candytuft 44
catkins 24, 26, 32
chain stitch 117, 121
clematis 44, 46
cluster stitches 120
collages
    Autumn Wreath 94–103
    Cottage Garden 34–43
    Flower Meadow 64–73
    Midsummer Daydream 54–63
    Midwinter Magic 104–13
    Poppy Posy 84–93
    Spring Awakening 24–33
    Terracotta Pot 74–83
    Vintage Blue Bouquet 44–53
    Woodland Glade 14–23
colour changes 40
containers 24, 27, 33, 46, 53, 84, 86
cornflower 84, 87, 90
cosmos 54, 57, 58
Cottage Garden (collage) 34–43
crab apple 94, 96, 99
crochet stitches 117–20

daffodil 24, 27, 29
daisy, ox-eye 34, 37, 39, 84, 86–8, 92
DC2TOG 119
double crochet stitch 118
double treble crochet stitch 119

echinacea 64, 67, 68
embroidery stitches 121

fennel 54, 57, 63
fern 14, 17, 21
Flower Meadow (collage) 64–73
forget-me-not 24, 26, 28
French knots 121

geranium 74, 76, 78
grape hyacinth 24, 27, 28
grasses 64, 66, 67, 73

half treble crochet stitch 118
hazel catkins 24, 26, 32
helenium 94, 97, 101
hellebore 14, 16, 20
hollyhock 34, 36, 40
hooks 11

inspiration 124–5
ivy 14, 16, 18

joins, invisible 120

lazy daisy stitch 121
leaves 17, 22–3, 26, 30, 36–9, 42, 44, 46,
    50, 56–7, 59, 63, 66, 71, 76–7, 80, 83, 86,
    92–3, 96–9, 101, 103–4, 107, 113
    see also fern; ivy
lichen 14, 17, 22
lily-of-the-valley 44, 47, 49

magic rings 117
marigold 74, 77, 80, 81
materials 10–11
Midsummer Daydream (collage)
    54–63
Midwinter Magic (collage) 104–13
mistletoe 107, 109
mushrooms 14, 17, 19, 94, 96, 100

peony 34, 37, 43
periwinkle 44, 46, 52
popcorn stitch 120

Poppy Posy (collage) 84–93
primrose 14, 17, 18
pussy willow 24, 26, 31

rose 34, 36, 41
rudbeckia 64, 66, 67, 71

scabious 44, 46, 48
scale 11
seedheads 44, 47, 51, 84, 87, 90
slipstitch 117
snowdrops 16, 20
Spring Awakening (collage) 24–33
stems 122
stiffening 122
stitches 117–21
straight stitch 121
sunflower 94, 97, 103

tails, sewing in multiple 123
techniques 115–23
Terracotta Pot (collage) 74–83
texture 123
three-dimensional motifs 123
toadstools 14, 17, 19, 94, 96, 100
tools 10–11
TR2TOG 119
treble crochet stitch 118
Triple Treble Crochet 119

variegated yarn 123
verbena 64, 67, 69
Vintage Blue Bouquet (collage) 44–53
violet 14, 16, 19

Woodland Glade (collage) 14–23

yarn 10–11, 123

ISBN-13: 9781446309391 paperback
ISBN-13: 9781446381885 EPUB
ISBN-13: 9781446310540 PDF

This book has been printed on paper from approved suppliers and
made from pulp from sustainable sources.

MIX
Paper from
responsible sources
FSC® C106499

Printed in Turkey by Omur for:
David and Charles, Ltd
Suite A, Tourism House, Pynes Hill, Exeter, EX2 5WS

10 9 8 7 6 5 4 3 2

Publishing Director: Ame Verso
Senior Commissioning Editor: Sarah Callard
Managing Editor: Jeni Chown
Editor: Jessica Cropper
Project Editors: Carol Ibbetson and Marie Clayton
Head of Design: Anna Wade
Design: Sam Staddon & Marieclare Mayne
Pre-press Designer: Ali Stark
Illustrations: Kuo Kang Chen
Art Direction: Sam Staddon
Photography: Jason Jenkins & Chris Norrington
Production Manager: Beverley Richardson

David and Charles publishes high-quality books on a wide range
of subjects. For more information visit **www.davidandcharles.com**

Share your makes with us on social media using **#dandcbooks**
and follow us on Facebook and Instagram by searching for
@dandcbooks

Layout of the digital edition of this book may vary depending on
reader hardware and display settings.